Barbara Whitney Petruzzelli, MLS
Editor

Real-Life Marketing and Promotion Strategies in College Libraries: Connecting with Campus and Community

Real-Life Marketing and Promotion Strategies in College Libraries: Connecting with Campus and Community has been co-published simultaneously as *College & Undergraduate Libraries*, Volume 12, Numbers 1/2 2005.

Pre-publication
REVIEWS,
COMMENTARIES,
EVALUATIONS . . .

More pre-publication
REVIEWS, COMMENTARIES, EVALUATIONS . . .

"A REFRESHINGLY PRACTICAL COMPILATION. . . . Provides A MOTHER LODE OF MARKETING RESOURCES–library and non-library, print and online. Many illustrations and tables reinforce the text. Noteworthy contributions outline the University of Northern British Columbia's multi-pronged promotional campaign, Texas A&M's collaboration with students to market and increase usage of e-books, and Tunxis Community College's annual fall theme party to celebrate patrons and promote services. This book is A GREAT STARTING POINT FOR ANY ACADEMIC LIBRARY'S MARKETING ACTIVITIES OR A SOURCE OF FRESH IDEAS FOR THE VETERAN PR LIBRARIAN."

Buff Hirko, AB, MLS
Statewide Virtual Reference
Project Coordinator
Washington State Library

"This book OFFERS A FRONT-ROW SEAT AT A MARKETING DISCUSSION ROUNDTABLE. Pull up a chair and be prepared to take notes as colleagues describe their academic library promotion journeys. AN EXCELLENT CHOICE for all those looking to jumpstart their promotion thinking and planning. Marketing teams, publicity organizations, and program planners seeking a fresh source of energy and counsel will find it worth their while to peruse this book. Librarians looking for inspiration will appreciate the swap meet of ideas they'll find in its pages. And marketing-savvy colleagues from other library settings will find themselves picking up strategies, pointers, and insights they can adapt to their own information service settings."

Chris Olson, MLS, MAS
Principal Consultant
Chris Olson & Associates

The Haworth Information Press®
An Imprint of The Haworth Press, Inc.

Real-Life Marketing and Promotion Strategies in College Libraries: Connecting with Campus and Community

Real-Life Marketing and Promotion Strategies in College Libraries: Connecting with Campus and Community has been co-published simultaneously as *College & Undergraduate Libraries*, Volume 12, Numbers 1/2 2005.

Monographic Separates from *College & Undergraduate Libraries*™

For additional information on these and other Haworth Press titles, including descriptions, tables of contents, reviews, and prices, use the QuickSearch catalog at http://www.HaworthPress.com.

Real-Life Marketing and Promotion Strategies in College Libraries: Connecting with Campus and Community, edited by Barbara Whitney Petruzzelli, MLS (Vol. 12, No. 1/2, 2005). *A how-to guide to marketing and promotional activities that will help academic libraries compete with other information providers.*

Future Teaching Roles for Academic Librarians, edited by Alice Harrison Bahr, PhD (Vol. 6, No. 2, 2000). *This vital guide examines current methods and suggestions on how to teach new technological developments to give patrons essential services and information.*

Real-Life Marketing and Promotion Strategies in College Libraries: Connecting with Campus and Community

Barbara Whitney Petruzzelli, MLS
Editor

Real-Life Marketing and Promotion Strategies in College Libraries: Connecting with Campus and Community has been co-published simultaneously as *College & Undergraduate Libraries*, Volume 12, Numbers 1/2 2005.

The Haworth Information Press®
An Imprint of The Haworth Press, Inc.

New York • London • Victoria (AU)
www.HaworthPress.com

Published by

The Haworth Information Press®, 10 Alice Street, Binghamton, NY 13904-1580 USA

The Haworth Information Press® is an imprint of The Haworth Press, Inc., 10 Alice Street, Binghamton, NY 13904-1580 USA.

Real-Life Marketing and Promotion Strategies in College Libraries: Connecting with Campus and Community has been co-published simultaneously as *College & Undergraduate Libraries*™, Volume 12, Numbers 1/2 2005.

Cover design by Kerry E. Mack.

Cover photo by Linda van der Zande, UNBC Office of Communications.

Library of Congress Cataloging-in-Publication Data

Real-life marketing and promotion strategies in college libraries : connecting with campus and community / Barbara Whitney Petruzzelli, editor.
     p. cm.
     "Co-published simultaneously as College & undergraduate libraries, volume 12, numbers 1/2 2005."
     Includes bibliographical references and index.
     ISBN-13: 978-0-7890-3157-0 (alk. paper)
     ISBN-10: 0-7890-3157-4 (alk. paper)
     ISBN-13: 978-0-7890-3158-7 (pbk. : alk. paper)
     ISBN-10: 0-7890-3158-2 (pbk. : alk. paper)
     1. Academic libraries–Marketing. 2. Academic libraries–Public relations. 3. Libraries and colleges. 4. Libraries and students. I. Petruzzelli, Barbara Whitney. II. College & undergraduate libraries.
Z716.3.R42 2005
025.1'977–dc22

2005023616

Indexing, Abstracting & Website/Internet Coverage

This section provides you with a list of major indexing & abstracting services and other tools for bibliographic access. That is to say, each service began covering this periodical during the year noted in the right column. Most Websites which are listed below have indicated that they will either post, disseminate, compile, archive, cite or alert their own Website users with research-based content from this work. (This list is as current as the copyright date of this publication.)

Abstracting, Website/Indexing Coverage . . . . Year When Coverage Began

- *Annual Bibliography of English Language & Literature*
  "Abstracts Section" (in print, CD-ROM, and online) 1999

- *Computer and Information Systems Abstracts*
  <http://www.csa.com> 2004

- *EBSCOhost Electronic Journals Service (EJS)*
  <http://ejournals.ebsco.com> 2001

- *Educational Administration Abstracts (EAA)* 1994

- *Google <http://www.google.com>* 2004

- *Google Scholar <http://scholar.google.com>* .2004

- *Haworth Document Delivery Center*
  <http://www.HaworthPress.com/journals/dds.asp> 1994

- *Higher Education Abstracts, providing the latest*
  in research & theory in more than 140 major topics 1994

- *IBZ International Bibliography of Periodical Literature*
  <http://www.saur.de> 1995

- *Index Guide to College Journals (core list compiled by integrating*
  48 indexes frequently used to support undergraduate
  programs in small to medium sized libraries) 1999

(continued)

(continued)

Special Bibliographic Notes related to special journal issues (separates) and indexing/abstracting:

- indexing/abstracting services in this list will also cover material in any "separate" that is co-published simultaneously with Haworth's special thematic journal issue or DocuSerial. Indexing/abstracting usually covers material at the article/chapter level.
- monographic co-editions are intended for either non-subscribers or libraries which intend to purchase a second copy for their circulating collections.
- monographic co-editions are reported to all jobbers/wholesalers/approval plans. The source journal is listed as the "series" to assist the prevention of duplicate purchasing in the same manner utilized for books-in-series.
- to facilitate user/access services all indexing/abstracting services are encouraged to utilize the co-indexing entry note indicated at the bottom of the first page of each article/chapter/contribution.
- this is intended to assist a library user of any reference tool (whether print, electronic, online, or CD-ROM) to locate the monographic version if the library has purchased this version but not a subscription to the source journal.
- individual articles/chapters in any Haworth publication are also available through the Haworth Document Delivery Service (HDDS).

Real-Life Marketing and Promotion Strategies in College Libraries: Connecting with Campus and Community

CONTENTS

ABOUT THE EDITOR

Barbara Whitney Petruzzelli is Associate Librarian and Assistant Library Director of the Sojourner Truth Library at the State University of New York at New Paltz. Her primary responsibilities include the marketing and promotion of library resources and services, which incorporates administering the Friends of the Sojourner Truth Library, leading library assessment efforts, coordinating the library liaison program, organizing special events, and producing the library newsletter and other promotional literature. Ms. Petruzzelli has ten years of previous work experience in marketing and sales support for several investment companies, serving as Vice President of Marketing Administration and Investor Communications at The Richard Roberts Group, Inc., as National Sales Director at The Meyers Group, Inc., and Director of Marketing and Investor Services at Security Data Group, Inc. She earned her M.L.S. degree from Syracuse University. Ms. Petruzzelli can be reached at Sojourner Truth Library, SUNY New Paltz, 75 S. Manheim Blvd., #3, New Paltz, NY 12561; address e-mail to petruzzb@newpaltz.edu.

Foreword

Pat Wagner

One practical way of tracking the concerns of academic library leadership is to note what in-house programs and consulting they request. Is an issue important enough to warrant a budget and the time of staff and managers? Ten years ago, no academic librarians were asking for classes on marketing, or assistance with the wording on a student survey, or help tweaking a promotional campaign, let alone requesting these topics for conferences. What a difference a decade makes.

Today, a workshop at an academic library conference with the word "marketing" in the title predictably will fill up fast. The attitude and sophistication of the attendees has changed as well. The necessity of promoting services, programming, collections, and web-based portals is a given. Most library staff members realize that both students and professors know they have choices besides the traditional library. They have

Pat Wagner and her husband Leif Smith own Pattern Research, Inc., a 30-year-old research and training enterprise based in Denver, Colorado. Ms. Wagner has worked with libraries since 1978 and is now one of the most sought-after consultants and trainers in library marketing, communications, and planning. Her presentations have been sponsored by ALA, ACRL, the LAMA/ALA Regional Institute, the Medical Library Association, the Special Libraries Association, and the Dynix Institute, among many others. She conducts classes and consults on marketing, media relations, strategic planning, project management, graphic design, community relations, ethical politics, and outreach to libraries of all types. Ms. Wagner has a background in graphic arts, radio, and print journalism, and earned a liberal arts degree with concentrations in print communication and performance. She can be reached at Pattern Research, PO Box 9100, Denver, CO 80209-0100 (address e-mail to: pat@pattern.com).

[Haworth co-indexing entry note]: "Foreword." Wagner, Pat. Co-published simultaneously in *College & Undergraduate Libraries* (The Haworth Information Press, an imprint of The Haworth Press, Inc.) Vol. 12, No. 1/2, 2005, pp. xxi-xxiv; and: *Real-Life Marketing and Promotion Strategies in College Libraries: Connecting with Campus and Community* (ed: Barbara Whitney Petruzzelli) The Haworth Information Press, an imprint of The Haworth Press, Inc., 2005, pp.xiii-xvi. Single or multiple copies of this article are available for a fee from The Haworth Document Delivery Service [1-800-HAWORTH, 9:00 a.m. - 5:00 p.m. (EST). E-mail address: docdelivery@haworthpress.com].

also learned that lecturing users on the superiority of consulting with professional librarians versus using the Internet for a quick search is usually futile. Participants in marketing programs are not only eager for new information, but also are happy to share expertise in everything from customer service training to evaluating the effectiveness of faculty intranets. Those experiences are the most valuable part of the class, as newcomers learn from peers.

The studies featured here represent the same marketing issues highlighted in the typical academic library marketing class, as well as the same generous spirit in terms of sharing specific practical examples to complement the theory. These marketing studies also mirror the journey that most participants take in their understanding of what marketing is, and how it relates to the mission of the modern academic library.

The first discovery participants make on the marketing journey is that marketing is much more than telling students and faculty about the latest bibliographic instruction class or promoting the value of research. Marketing begins and ends with awareness of the library's users: their values, their concerns, the world from their points of view. Marketing is a conversation, where the library customer does 75% of the talking.

This conversation needs to be an ongoing process, using different assessment tools. One of the most valuable tools is the focus group, where students and faculty share their views with library staff. User feedback can be painful, but the reward is a library that is relevant to their needs. Focus groups, surveys, and observations also capture valuable clues about improving the effectiveness of promotional materials. Do commuter students and faculty listen to the campus radio station? Will direct mail work better than flyers in the hallways? If you don't ask, you will never know. And the dialog is ongoing. No matter how well you think you are promoting the library, you must always ask the user: Are you getting what you want? How are we doing?

The second discovery that library marketing students will make is the necessity of persistence. When the promotional stage of marketing the academic library finally kicks in, it never ends. It is a process that is 24/7, 365 days, 360 degrees.

Marketing is communication. It is the equivalent of the nervous system of the institution. Data is received through observation and measurement. If the organism—or institution—is healthy, it responds quickly and appropriately to the input it receives, whether it is the heat of a hot stove on an unsuspecting finger or complaints of students about inadequate seating in the study areas. Reaching out to the entire academic community with theme parties that can dispel stuffy stereotypes sends a message about the identity of the academic library. The importance of such messages cannot be taken for granted; classic marketing principles apply to state-of-the-art services, such as virtual reference, as well as to physical collections.

The third discovery on the journey to becoming adept at marketing academic libraries is that there are an almost infinite array of tools available and places to start. Because feeling overwhelmed can freeze the neophyte into a stasis of planning and meetings (but no execution), it is very useful to know where to start. Fortunately, academic libraries already have ready-made resources available to jumpstart the process, including the American Library Association's "@ your library" campaign.

Marketing class participants also learn that the little things count. A simple postcard can be more effective than wordy flyers. And many successful marketing efforts are based on the premise that the library is understaffed with a limited budget. Marketing strategies do not have to elaborate and they can fit into the stressed out academic library workplace. Knowing that other academic libraries have built their marketing success one small step at a time is one of the best antidotes for the "frozen-in-the-headlights" syndrome.

The fourth discovery on the journey is that marketing is an activity that is done with other people and institutions. The lone eagle will not be as successful as the person who sees partners and opportunities everywhere and takes advantages of potential connections for mutual benefit. Academic libraries can extend their marketing efforts beyond their fingertips by collaborating and communicating beyond the halls of academe to the greater community. The library user, specifically the students, can partner with the library staff in creating successful advertising campaigns. And, at the most basic level of good librarianship, academic librarians need to assume that others have cleared the path. Books and websites flag best practices; the sharing continues after class. The burden is shared.

The last discovery that the participants in a class on marketing libraries will make is that marketing is an experiment. Do the research and execute the plan, but understand that success is not a given. Hopefully, each failure is a source of data for future improvements, but the final truth is that marketing is risky and often you get to make mistakes in front of a critical public. But the choice is stagnation and a slow decline. A current popular e-mail signature line, attributed to a book by management guru Tom Peters, sums up the issue nicely: If you don't like change, you will like irrelevance even less.

Building great collections and online services are not enough. Without the willingness to listen to library users, act on their feedback, and communicate the benefits of the modern academic library to the people you serve, libraries will become the anachronisms their critics are predicting. Fortunately, you have guides to help you on your journey. The first step is yours to take.

Using Student Focus Groups to Inform Library Planning and Marketing

Melissa L. Becher

Janice L. Flug

SUMMARY. American University Library participated in the LibQUAL+ survey of library service quality sponsored by the Association of Research Libraries. Upon analyzing the results, the library's Assessment Team decided to engage in follow-up assessment in order to gain a better understanding of undergraduate perceptions of and priorities for library service. The team conducted three focus groups of randomly selected undergraduate students. This article addresses the team's methodology, implementation, and results of the focus group study. It also describes how the results of LibQUAL+, the focus groups, and other assessment activities are being incorporated into the library's short- and long-range planning and marketing activities. *[Article copies available for a fee from The Haworth Document Delivery Service: 1-800-HAWORTH. E-mail address: <docdelivery@haworthpress.com> Website: <http://www.HaworthPress.com> © 2005 by The Haworth Press, Inc. All rights reserved.]*

Melissa L. Becher (MSLIS, University of Illinois at Urbana-Champaign) is Reference and Instruction Librarian, American University Library, 4400 Massachusetts Avenue, N.W., Washington, DC 20016-8046 (address e-mail to: mbecher@american. edu).

Janice L. Flug (MLS, University of Maryland) is Acquisitions Librarian, American University Library, 4400 Massachusetts Avenue, N.W., Washington, DC 20016-8046 (address e-mail to: jflug@american.edu).

[Haworth co-indexing entry note]: "Using Student Focus Groups to Inform Library Planning and Marketing." Becher, Melissa L., and Janice L. Flug. Co-published simultaneously in *College & Undergraduate Libraries* (The Haworth Information Press, an imprint of The Haworth Press, Inc.) Vol. 12, No. 1/2, 2005, pp. 1-18; and: *Real-Life Marketing and Promotion Strategies in College Libraries: Connecting with Campus and Community* (ed: Barbara Whitney Petruzzelli) The Haworth Information Press, an imprint of The Haworth Press, Inc., 2005, pp. 1-18. Single or multiple copies of this article are available for a fee from The Haworth Document Delivery Service [1-800-HAWORTH, 9:00 a.m. - 5:00 p.m. (EST). E-mail address: docdelivery@haworthpress.com].

1

KEYWORDS. Library assessment, focus groups, library planning, library marketing, LibQUAL+

As assessment becomes more prominent in higher education, academic libraries are increasingly bringing their services under scrutiny through user surveys and other assessment tools. These projects help librarians determine what users need, how well the library is meeting those needs, and how improvements in service can be made.

Assessment cannot be looked at as a one-time event, but should be incorporated into the library's on-going activities. One user study cannot provide definitive information about what the user population wants. There could be an anomaly that skews the results. Instead of relying on one kind of assessment, the library should use different tools to assess its services and should repeat studies at regular intervals. In this way, a trend of responses emerges that gives library staff confidence that they correctly understand users' expectations.

Beyond simply administering assessment tools, libraries must be prepared to act on assessment results. Assessment should be linked both to planning cycles, so that improvements identified by users are actually made, and to marketing efforts, so that users are aware that the library is responding to their needs. When planning for multiple surveys of the same users over time, it is particularly important that they know their opinions are being heard and addressed.

This article illustrates how American University Library has implemented a culture of assessment to gain knowledge of user needs and to use this knowledge to inform planning and marketing strategies. A series of focus group studies of undergraduate students was conducted by the library in the fall of 2002. The need for these focus groups emerged from another assessment project, participation in the LibQUAL+ library service quality survey. The results of the focus groups have been incorporated into library planning and into an emerging marketing campaign.

American University is located in Washington, DC. The student body consists of just under 6,000 undergraduates and approximately 3,500 graduate students. Students come from every state and over 150 countries. The university offers courses through its colleges and schools, including arts and sciences, business, education, public affairs, international service, and communication. Additionally, there is a law school with a separate user base and a library to serve it.

American University Library has integrated support for assessment projects into its organizational structure. In the spring of 1999, the library reorganized into a team environment. The first team formed was a Management Team made up of library administrators and elected representatives from the library faculty and staff. This team subsequently created an Assessment Team made up of members from the Management Team and other interested individuals.[1] The initial mission of the Assessment Team was to evaluate the reorganization, but the Team quickly moved on to surveying users about their perceptions of the library and library services, as well as their desires for other library services. The current Team is made up of two library faculty members, three library staff members, and the University Librarian; it conducts one or two major assessment projects a year. The Team has helped infuse assessment into the culture of the library and ensures that a number of library staff are constantly analyzing the "big picture" of how American University students and faculty perceive the library and its services.

BACKGROUND:
LIBQUAL+ AND FOCUS GROUPS

American University (AU) Library participated in the LibQUAL+ survey in Spring 2001. LibQUAL+ is an effort sponsored by the Association of Research Libraries (ARL) to measure service quality and to identify best practices in university libraries. AU was one of 44 institutions that participated in year one of the project. Subsequently, the library has participated in LibQUAL+ 2003 and 2005 surveys.[2] The American University Library Assessment Team facilitated the administration of the survey and analyzed the findings. Undergraduate and graduate students, as well as faculty, participated in the survey.

The 2001 instrument included fifty-six service level questions; in addition each respondent was asked a few demographic questions. Respondents were randomly presented with one of two versions of the questionnaire. The short version asked the respondent to select the level of perceived service the library was providing based upon a nine-point scale. The longer version asked the respondent to select not only the level of perceived service for each question, but also the minimum level of acceptable service *and* their desired level of service. The range between the minimum and desired levels of service is called the range of tolerance.

The library service issues covered by LibQUAL+ were categorized into nine dimensions: *Access to Collections, Assurance, Empathy, Library as Place, Reliability, Responsiveness, Tangibles, Self-Reliance,* and *Instruction.*

The findings of the LibQUAL+ survey were made available to participating libraries in early summer 2001. Three dimensions emerged as sources of major concern to the AU community: Access to Collections, Library as Place, and Reliability. These three had the greatest negative gaps between the minimum and perceived levels of service. Particularly striking were the results from undergraduate students. One-hundred-ninety undergraduates completed the survey. Of the fifty-six service level questions, only six scored within the range of tolerance; these were the questions pertaining to instruction. LibQUAL+ results demonstrated that American University Library was not meeting many of the minimum expectations of undergraduate students. However, due to the broad, general nature of the questions, it was difficult to isolate specific areas of dissatisfaction. The Assessment Team needed a better understanding of the results before sharing them with other library teams or putting forth recommendations.

LibQUAL+ provided the quantitative analysis. In order to discover what the numbers meant and to provide direction for the library, qualitative information was also needed. According to Richard Krueger (1994, 29), "researchers are recognizing the benefits of combining qualitative and quantitative procedures, resulting in greater methodological mixes that strengthen the research design." ARL's LibQUAL+ training stressed that libraries should not rely on just one method of data gathering. In a review of the literature, several authors noted the value of using focus groups to assist in interpreting quantitative data (Widdows 1991). Focus groups allow for exploring and obtaining an in-depth knowledge of users' perceptions, desires, expectations, and experiences (Crowley 2002). As noted in several articles on focus groups in library research, the business sector commonly employs focus groups as a market research tool. Applied social scientists began using focus groups over sixty years ago (Crowley 2002). In the last ten to fifteen years, there has been more pressure on libraries to assess their services. At approximately the same time, library research began to incorporate focus groups. Pairing the specific information gained from focus groups with the quantitative data generated by surveys allows librarians to gain deeper insight into issues facing the library.

The Assessment Team recommended to the Management Team that the library conduct focus groups of undergraduate students in an attempt to better comprehend their perceptions of the library and also to test some hypotheses about why their LibQUAL+ ratings were lower than those reported by graduate students. Further, the Team wanted to explore how well the library was promoting its services.

The goal of a focus group is to have participants who are similar to each other expressing their opinions about an issue, as well as reacting to the viewpoints of others. Some participants may not know how to express their feelings toward a service issue until they hear others' opinions (Krueger 1994). The focus group interview can vary in the level of structure; this will differ depending upon the research design. In order to detect patterns or trends, there must be enough similarity between the groups with respect to participants (Crowley 2002). Since the number of participants in the set of focus groups will be limited, care must be taken not to use this data to generalize to the larger population.

Implementing a focus group study can be challenging. The first step must be to determine the research objectives. Equally important is identifying which group will be recruited (Edmunds 1989). Other issues to be addressed include how many group sessions will be held, who will conduct the sessions, and how the data will be analyzed and used (Crowley 2002). The mere act of holding focus group sessions can be a good public relations tool for the library (Massey-Burzio 1998).

METHODOLOGY

In putting the focus groups together, the Library Assessment Team relied heavily on advice from the university's Office of Institutional Research and Assessment. The director of the office was very enthusiastic about the library's project, and provided advice on coordinating participation in the focus groups, devising questions to ask, and analyzing the results. She also agreed to serve as a facilitator for all three focus groups to provide a neutral atmosphere in which students would be comfortable expressing their opinions. Her experience with leading groups of this type was invaluable to the success of the project.

The focus groups were assembled from undergraduate students randomly selected from the student database by the university Registrar's Office. Six hundred e-mail addresses were provided, from which the systems librarian constructed a mailing list. Invitations to take part in the focus groups were sent to all 600 students in the sample. A separate e-mail account was established for the invitations, so that invitations would not come from any one individual's e-mail account. Invitations included a description of the event, a choice of dates and times, and a promise of pizza and cookies.

Sixty students, or ten percent of those invited, responded to the invitation, and the Assessment Team Leader matched them up with three sessions scheduled for late fall. In the end, twenty-six undergraduates participated. Two sessions had eight students and one had ten, both reasonable numbers for focus group sessions (Crowley 2002, 207).

The sessions were held in the student union, again to provide a neutral atmosphere for true exchange of opinions. Each session was recorded on audiotape. Student identities were protected by assigning numbers upon arrival and referring to those numbers throughout the session. A member of the Assessment Team was present at the sessions, but sat at the back of the room and remained a silent observer.

The format of the sessions took students through a logical progression of thinking about the library's services. At the beginning of each session, students were asked to rate the library overall on a scale from one to ten and to write down their reasons for giving the rating they did (see Appendix A). Then, the facilitator led a discussion in which the reasons the students gave were compiled into eight Library Quality Indicators. Students were then asked to rank the Quality Indicators in order of importance and to indicate their level of satisfaction with the library on each one (see Appendix B). A second topic of discussion brought out why students considered certain factors more important than others and why they rated the library at a certain overall level of satisfaction. The format of the program provided a lot of detailed information about student perceptions of the library and why students felt the way they did.

At the end of the sessions, students filled out a general questionnaire in which they indicated how satisfied they were with individual service desks on a scale from one to ten (see Appendix C). They also were asked to agree or disagree with statements about the library such as "the library materials I need are usually checked out" and "I use the library as a place of study" (see Appendix D). Students again identified themselves on the questionnaires by number, so that the questionnaire answers could be linked to elements of the discussion without identifying individuals.

In addition to the enticement of food, the library offered other incentives for participating in the focus groups. Each student was given a no-spill mug of the type permitted in the library for beverages. The Assessment Team also hid free $25 printing cards for the library's laser printers in two of the mugs for each session.

DATA ANALYSIS

The Assessment Team listened to the audio tapes of the sessions, shared the notes of the sessions, and conducted a review of all the questionnaires. Since some parts of the focus group interview were open-ended or unstructured, the three sessions could not be compared on a one-to-one basis. The unstructured questions provided the Team with a rich amount of data about the undergraduate library experience. The first task was to find trends and patterns. Four common Library Quality Indicators were clearly detectable from all three focus groups: The Collection, The Physical Environment, ALADIN (our online catalog)/Online Resources, and Librarians/Customer Service. The Team was confident that it could generalize across the focus groups for these four areas. These four indicators also closely paralleled the results of the LibQUAL+ survey, which gave the Team some confidence that they could be generalized to the user population as a whole.

The Collection was rated as the highest in importance by the students. On an 8-point scale with 1 being the highest, the Collection received an average rating of 2. Students in general responded positively to the Washington Research Library Consortium which gives them the ability to obtain books from other libraries. However, from their comments, it was clear that students want more books to be available to them on-site. A number of students expressed disappointment that the books listed in ALADIN as being owned by AU were not actually on the shelf. Others stated that the consortium loan service sometimes could not get the item needed or could not get it fast enough. A few posited that AU relies too heavily on the consortium and that it is used to justify an inadequate budget. There were some positive comments, as well, citing specific subject areas of the collection and the ability to access electronic journals.

The students participating in the focus groups stated that they want:

- a larger collection; more new books in certain areas
- gaps in parts of the collection to be filled
- the ability to check out media (only faculty can borrow media)
- more material on e-Reserves
- a clearer classification or arrangement of library books

The Physical Environment was second in importance, receiving a ranking of 3.7. Students were generally positive about the level of technology available in the library. The number of computers and network ports appeared to meet their needs. However, in general, students found that the library's physical environment was uncomfortable enough to preclude studying there.

Specific areas of student concern were lighting, temperature, comfort of furniture, noise level, group study space, and the layout of the library. Undergraduates' perceptions and expectations of Library as Place in the LibQUAL+ survey corresponded closely with the more specific views expressed in the focus groups.

ALADIN/Online Resources was the third Library Quality Indicator. Within and between the focus groups there was not a clear definition of what was included in this descriptor. Sometimes there seemed to be a blur between students' perceptions of the Web and the library's own electronic resources.

Generally the students offered positive comments about electronic resources. The library's databases were adequate for their research purposes. Students appreciated being able to get books and articles from other schools by submitting electronic requests; however, some stated that they would not use this service because the materials should be available on-site. Some students had trouble finding electronic journals and running searches in electronic resources. The Assessment Team thought that the search difficulties could be an instructional issue.

The final common Library Quality Indicator was what the Team labeled Librarians/Customer Service. This indicator generated both positive and negative comments. While some said that help at the library was "excellent" and made them feel very comfortable, others said that the instruction they got was too basic or was too focused on giving an answer rather than teaching the student how to find the information. There were no specifics on service desks or positions. Some students who had attended library instruction classes were very happy with them, while others were not aware that there were library instruction classes. Several students stated that they wanted to "do it myself" without intervention from a librarian.

The focus groups offered the Assessment Team an opportunity to delve more deeply into some of the issues raised in the LibQUAL+ survey. The Team was able to isolate more precisely what dissatisfied undergraduate students and what they would like to see changed.

APPLICATION OF FOCUS GROUP FINDINGS

The efforts of the Assessment Team have a significant impact on American University Library's planning process. Findings and recommendations are shared throughout the library and with university administrators. Members of the Assessment Team are currently on the Library Management Team and the Strategic Planning Team. This facilitates a flow of information from assessment activities to the main planning groups in the library and encourages other library teams to use the findings from the surveys and focus groups.

Here are some specific examples of how focus group findings have been used in library planning and marketing, and in campus-wide initiatives:

In Spring 2003, the library's Strategic Planning Team assembled information and set possible priorities for the library to focus on for the next two years. Concepts and comments from the focus group report, along with other data and resources, were used by the library faculty and staff to prioritize potential initiatives.

The comments and concerns expressed by the undergraduate students, while not new, helped to clarify service issues and reminded library faculty and staff not to assume they knew what students wanted or needed. For example, both the arrangement of the book stacks and the need for more books on-site were concerns raised in the focus groups. As a result, reconfiguring the stacks to create a more logical arrangement and to accommodate a larger portion of the collection emerged as a top priority. The priorities established at the planning sessions then became a part of the Library Action Plan 2003-2004. During summer 2004, the library re-oriented the stacks, shifted the collection, installed additional shelving, purchased new couches and armchairs, and installed new carpeting.

While the Action Plan represents short-term planning, the AU Library is also working toward several long-range goals. One of the most expensive and challenging goals is the expansion of the library building. Annually, the university conducts a Campus Climate Survey, asking students five or six questions concerning service quality for each major office or department, including the library. The results of the LibQUAL+ survey, Campus Climate Surveys, and the focus groups reinforced the view that our physical space must be addressed in the near future. They provided evidence that students feel strongly about the physical presence of the library and desire more room for group study and collections. The library makes a stronger case to university administration for an expanded building when it's based on assessment outcomes.

The results of the survey and focus group findings have also provided a more clearly defined platform from which to involve student leaders in long-range planning for the library. In the past, priorities changed with each election of new student leaders. As a result of assessment findings underpinning our long-range planning, there is more consistency from year to year in the issues that we seek to work on together.

More recently, results from the 2001 and 2003 LibQUAL+ surveys, the Campus Climate Surveys, and the focus groups were used in the development of a library marketing campaign targeted at undergraduates. A proposal to form a new Marketing Team described the team's proposed work as "the logical outcome of the work done by the Assessment Team." The Assessment Team shared with the Marketing Team the results of the 2003 LibQUAL+ survey and compared the results with the 2001 survey and the focus groups. Largely based upon this assessment information, the Team designed a marketing campaign focused on enhancing undergraduates' knowledge of library services. The Assessment Team is now awaiting the results of the 2005 LibQUAL+ survey to see if the campaign has had an impact on the rankings. With the formation of the Marketing Team, the cycle of assessment, planning, implementation of changes, and marketing is now formally in place at the library.

Finally, American University has just completed a self-study as part of the Middle States Association of Colleges and Schools accreditation review. The new evaluation criteria include an emphasis on assessment. Since the library is one of the campus units that has undertaken innovative assessment projects, some of the findings from the LibQUAL+ survey and the focus groups are included in the report. The findings are used to highlight the positive aspects of library service and also to identify library services and facilities that could be strengthened or enhanced.

In response to the report and the accreditation visit, American University created a project team to follow up on assessment issues, particularly the development and assessment of learning outcomes for each school and college. The library's Assessment Team leader has a seat on this team and is well-placed to involve the library in further campus-wide assessment efforts.

REFLECTIONS ON FOCUS GROUPS AND ASSESSMENT

The focus groups conducted by the Assessment Team in the fall of 2002 were the first foray into the use of "live" assessment tools by the

Team. The decision to use the focus group approach to obtain more specificity on several issues and with a defined category of users was not a casual one. It is critical to decide upon clear objectives desired as a result of using focus groups. It is also important to have a limited number of objectives for the focus groups so the discussion topics can be explored at length. Since facilitation expertise may be limited within the library, it can be helpful to take advantage of local experts and resources. Most colleges and universities have offices similar to American University's Office of Institutional Research and Assessment. We found it invaluable to seek the director's insights and guidance on this and other assessment projects. Plus, her neutrality as focus group facilitator allowed for a better flow of information during the sessions.

The combination of structured and unstructured questions provided the undergraduate students several ways in which to express their thoughts. It also gave the participants an opportunity to hear what classmates were thinking. Most importantly, the combination of written evaluations and discussion, captured on audio tape, provided the Assessment Team with a rich source of data. The demographic data gathered also provided the Team with additional analysis variables. Using a combination of data gathering methods allows for differences in participants' communication styles and comfort levels.

Even though the data gathered in the focus groups provided insights into the perception of library service and the needs of some undergraduate students, caution must be exercised in trying to use a small sample to generalize results too broadly, possibly magnifying negative statements and then over-responding. The Team felt comfortable in generalizing about some aspects of the focus groups but only in combination with the LibQUAL+ and Campus Climate Survey results. One assessment survey or tool alone cannot provide a complete picture. By participating in LibQUAL+ or similar surveys, it is possible to establish benchmarks for the individual library and for comparison with similar libraries.

Since AU's Library Assessment Team began operating about five years ago, library faculty and staff have become more comfortable with the data obtained during an assessment activity. It is difficult not to be defensive when the library receives criticism from its users. The use of a neutral facilitator will prevent inadvertent defensiveness during the focus group sessions. Both positive ratings and comments, along with negatives, will be obtained from any assessment activity. The best approach is to be ready to build upon the positive and use criticism to improve library services.

Another common reaction to assessment initiatives is the assumption that library staff members already know what the users want or need. This assumption will not serve the library well. As quickly as information formats and access to information changes, the desires and needs of the library user change. Further, expressed needs are most likely to be different from one institution to another. Therefore, a service that excels at one library may be totally wrong for another. The only way to know is to ask. And once an answer is given, the library must be prepared to act.

Assessment data must be shared internally with library staff, particularly with those involved in planning and marketing, and externally with university administrators, faculty, and students. The library will need the assistance of the parent organization in order to implement major changes. AU library administration has effectively used assessment data in the annual budget request, resulting in increased funding for library collections and technology, as well as funds for the library stacks project.

Finally, assessment is a continuous process. Change is constant, and evaluating library services must also be on-going. However, care must be taken that the user population can see changes as a result of their responses during the assessment process, so that library assessment efforts are seen as credible and worth their participation. The relationship between assessment, planning, implementation, and marketing of library services can play a critical role in how the library is perceived.

In the past several years, the AU library has become more organized in its assessment and marketing activities. By using assessment instruments, it is possible to focus on consistent themes with sufficient data to provide foundation. Our constituencies recognize the library's willingness to listen and implement improvements and enhancements based upon user comments and rankings. Student groups and faculty have become partners in voicing support for increased resources for the library, particularly to enhance library collections. The university administration and the board of trustees include the library as one of their budget priorities. Library planning has become more sophisticated and we are more confident that the appropriate issues are being addressed. Short- and long-range plans are largely based upon the results of assessment projects. Once new assessment results are available, the library's goals and objectives are reviewed and revised. It is now second-nature to have confirmation from our user groups for decisions and new directions.

QUICK BIB

Crowley, Gwyneth H., Rob Leffel, Diana Ramirez and others. 2002 "User perception of the library web pages: a focus group study at Texas A&M University." *The Journal of Academic Librarianship* 28: 205-210.

Edmunds, H. 1999 *The focus groups research handbook*. Chicago: NTC Business Books.

Krueger, R.A. 1994 *Focus groups: a practical guide for applied research*. 2nd ed. Thousand Oaks, CA: Sage Publication.

Widdows, Richard, Tia A. Hensler and Marlaya H. Wyncott. 1991 "The focus group interview: a method for assessing users' evaluation of library service." *College & Research Libraries* 52: 352-359.

NOTES

1. The authors wish to acknowledge the other members of the American University Library Assessment Team who participated in the focus group project, including the analysis and report writing. The Team members were: Patricia Wand, University Librarian; Eve Steinberger, Database Management Specialist; and Richard Mereand, Reference Electronic Resources Assistant. The authors also acknowledge the contributions and guidance of Karen Froslid-Jones, Director of the American University Office of Institutional Research and Assessment.

2. The results of the LibQUAL+ 2003 survey generally reinforced the information gathered using earlier assessment tools. Overall, the 2003 rankings were not as negative as the 2001 rankings; even the undergraduate rankings were more gratifying. This may be due in part to an improved assessment instrument.

REFERENCES

Crowley, Gwyneth H., Rob Leffel, Diana Ramirez and others. 2002 "User perceptions of the library web pages: a focus group study at Texas A&M University." *The Journal of Academic Librarianship* 28: 205-210.

Edmunds, H. 1999 *The focus groups research handbook*. Chicago: NTC Business Books.

Krueger, R.A. 1994 *Focus groups: a practical guide for applied research*. 2nd ed. Thousand Oaks, CA: Sage Publications.

Massey-Burzio, Virginia. 1998 "From the other side of the reference desk: a focus group study." *The Journal of Academic Librarianship* 24:208-15.

Widdows, Richard, Tia A. Hensler and Marlaya H. Wyncott. 1991 "The focus group interview: a method for assessing users' evaluation of library service." *College & Research Libraries* 52:352-359.

ADDITIONAL RESOURCES

Cook, Colleen, Fred M. Heath and Bruce Thompson. 2001 "LibQUAL+: one instrument in the new measures toolbox." *Journal of Library Administration* 35: 41-46.

Glitz, Beryl. 1997 "The focus group technique in library research: an introduction." *Bulletin of Medical Library Association* 85: 385-390.

Ho, Jeannette and Gwyneth H. Crowley. 2003 "User perceptions of the "reliability" of library services at Texas A&M University: focus group study." *The Journal of Academic Librarianship* 29: 82-87.

Huff-Eibl, Robyn and Shelley Phipps. 2002 "Using LibQUAL+ results at the University of Arizona: responding to customer input–listening and acting." *ARL* 221: 12-13.

Kemp, Jan H. 2001 "Using the LibQUAL+ Survey to Assess User Perceptions of Collections and Service Quality." *Collection Management* 26: 1-14.

Kerslake, Evelyn and Anne Goulding. 1996 "Focus groups: their use in LIS research data collection." *Education for Information* 14: 225-232.

Perry, Valerie E. 2002 "Putting knowledge to work effectively: assessing information needs through focus groups." *INSPEL* 36: 254-265.

Waller, Consuella Askew and Kaylyn E. Hipps. 2002 "Using LibQUAL+ and developing a culture of assessment in libraries." *ARL* 221: 10-11.

Young, Nancy J. and Marilyn Von Seggern. 2001 "General information seeking in changing times: a focus group study." *Reference & User Services Quarterly* 41: 159-169.

APPENDIX A. Focus Group Participant Data Sheet and Overall Satisfaction
Question

LIBRARY FOCUS GROUP QUESTIONS

Number: _____

School/College: CAS   SOC   SPA   SIS   KSB

Primary Major: _____

Gender: M   F

Class: Fresh. Soph. Jr. Sr.

Overall, how satisfied are you with the University Library?

Very Dissatisfied   Very Satisfied

1   2   3   4   5   6   7   8   9   10

Why did you give it the rating that you did?

_____

_____

_____

_____

_____

_____

_____

_____

APPENDIX B. Quality Indicators Ranking Sheet

BENDER LIBRARY FOCUS GROUP

Number: _____

Importance Rank	Level of Satisfaction (1-10)	Bender Library Quality Indicators
_____	_____	_____
_____	_____	_____
_____	_____	_____
_____	_____	_____
_____	_____	_____
_____	_____	_____
_____	_____	_____
_____	_____	_____

APPENDIX C. Service Desk Satisfaction Questions

Number: _____

Overall, how satisfied are you with the reference desk assistance provided by Bender Library?

Very Dissatisfied   Very Satisfied
  1   2   3   4   5   6   7   8   9   10

Overall, how satisfied are you with the reserve services provided by Bender Library?

Very Dissatisfied   Very Satisfied
  1   2   3   4   5   6   7   8   9   10

Overall, how satisfied are you with the materials (quality and quantity of books, etc.) in Bender Library?

Very Dissatisfied   Very Satisfied
  1   2   3   4   5   6   7   8   9   10

Overall, how satisfied are you with the inter-library loan service provided by Bender Library?

Very Dissatisfied   Very Satisfied
  1   2   3   4   5   6   7   8   9   10

Overall, how satisfied are you with the services provided by the circulation desk?

Very Dissatisfied   Very Satisfied
  1   2   3   4   5   6   7   8   9   10

Overall, how satisfied are you with the on-line research tools?

Very Dissatisfied   Very Satisfied
  1   2   3   4   5   6   7   8   9   10

Overall, how satisfied are you with the Facilities (study space, etc.) at Bender Library?

Very Dissatisfied   Very Satisfied
  1   2   3   4   5   6   7   8   9   10

APPENDIX D. Library Use and Satisfaction Questions

LIBRARY FOCUS GROUP

Number: _____

Please answer the following questions:
(SA = Stronly Agree, A = Agree, D = Disagreee, SD = Strongly Disagree, NA = Not Applicable)

I use the library as a place to study.   SA   A   D   SD   NA

I regularly ask the reference librarians   SA   A   D   SD   NA
for help when I can't find what I need.

I feel confident that I know how to use   SA   A   D   SD   NA
Aladin to find the materials that I need.

I can easily find the information that I need.   SA   A   D   SD   NA

I feel confident that I know how to obtain   SA   A   D   SD   NA
material if it is not available in Bender Library.

I use inter-library loan when A.U. doesn't   SA   A   D   SD   NA
have the material that I need.

I have had articles e-mailed to me using   SA   A   D   SD   NA
Aladin.

The A.U. materials I need are usually   SA   A   D   SD   NA
checked out.

The materials I need are usually at another   SA   A   D   SD   NA
library.

The materials I need are not available in   SA   A   D   SD   NA
Aladin.

In general, I am satisfied with the way in   SA   A   D   SD   NA
which I am treated at the library.

In general, I am satisfied with library support   SA   A   D   SD   NA
for my learning, research and teaching needs.

I generally do the bulk of my library research:

____ 1-3 days before a project is due.
____ 4-6 days before a project is due.
____ 7-10 days before a project is due.
____ 11-13 days before a project is due.
____ 2-4 weeks before a project is due.
____ more than a month before my project is due.

Marketing the Academic Library: Building on the "@ your library" Framework

Heather Empey
Nancy E. Black

SUMMARY. Academic libraries do not often launch public relations campaigns. However, recent changes and enhancements at the Geoffrey R. Weller Library at the University of Northern British Columbia prompted librarians to embark on a public awareness campaign built upon the "@ your library" framework. The campaign featured multiple strategies, including posters, displays, brochures, newspaper ads, and giveaways. The goal of the campaign was to break away from the stereotypical image of the library as a research necessity, and show it instead as the beating heart of the University. The campaign is evaluated and the continued need for marketing and promotion of academic library services is examined. *[Article copies available for a fee from The Haworth Document Delivery Service: 1-800-HAWORTH. E-mail address: <docdelivery@haworthpress.com> Website: <http://www.HaworthPress.com> © 2005 by The Haworth Press, Inc. All rights reserved.]*

Heather Empey (MLIS, University of Alberta) is Education Librarian, University of Northern British Columbia, 3333 University Way, Prince George, BC, V2N 4Z9, Canada (address e-mail to: empeyh@unbc.ca).

Nancy E. Black (MLS, Dalhousie University) is Distance & Document Delivery Librarian, University of Northern British Columbia, 3333 University Way, Prince George, BC, V2N 4Z9, Canada (address e-mail to: blackn@unbc.ca).

[Haworth co-indexing entry note]: "Marketing the Academic Library: Building on the "@ your library" Framework." Empey, Heather, and Nancy E. Black. Co-published simultaneously in *College & Undergraduate Libraries* (The Haworth Information Press, an imprint of The Haworth Press, Inc.) Vol. 12, No. 1/2, 2005, pp. 19-33; and: *Real-Life Marketing and Promotion Strategies in College Libraries: Connecting with Campus and Community* (ed: Barbara Whitney Petruzzelli) The Haworth Information Press, an imprint of The Haworth Press, Inc., 2005, pp. 19-33. Single or multiple copies of this article are available for a fee from The Haworth Document Delivery Service [1-800-HAWORTH, 9:00 a.m. - 5:00 p.m. (EST). E-mail address: docdelivery@haworthpress.com].

Available online at http://www.haworthpress.com/web/CUL
© 2005 by The Haworth Press, Inc. All rights reserved.
doi:10.1300/J106v12n01_02

KEYWORDS. Marketing, public relations campaigns, academic libraries, @ your library

INTRODUCTION

Opened in 1994, the University of Northern British Columbia (UNBC) in Prince George, British Columbia, is Canada's newest university. Approximately 3,500 students attend UNBC, including roughly 350 distance students predominantly from the northern regions of the province. In addition to a wide variety of bachelor's degrees, UNBC offers several master's degrees and two Ph.D. programs.

From the beginning, the institution has been recognized for its innovation, both in marketing strategies and in academic strength. The citizens of this northern community, for example, were so eager to establish a university that thousands of people paid five dollars each in the late 1980s-early 1990s to support its creation. At several graduation ceremonies, the graduating class has been invited to stand so everyone can see "What their 5 bucks paid for." Visually, this is a moving and dramatic moment during the ceremony and speaks to the power of marketing.

With respect to the university's academic strength, evidence comes from the annual Maclean's ranking of Canadian universities (Rankings 2004). In 1998, within five years of its official opening, UNBC ranked among the top ten of 21 undergraduate universities in Canada (Black 2001), a ranking still held by the university.

In this environment of innovation, the Geoffrey R. Weller Library (named for UNBC's founding president), is a stunning architectural showpiece as well as an excellent library heavily used by students and faculty. (The building is featured on the cover of the October 2003 issue of *Choice.*) Due to its position of status on campus, Weller Library is always included on university tours for the general public, school groups, and prospective faculty. In this respect, Weller Library fulfills the value of "brand identity" as noted by Wolpert (1998); that is, the library as a building is recognized for its inspiring presence.

However, despite its status and brand identity, library resources, services, and staff were not always appreciated, valued, or understood. Concerns about library services were communicated consistently to library personnel through both informal (such as general comments, questions, complaints) and formal (institutional meetings) avenues. The feedback included comments about service standards, lack of resources, and finally, the sense that no one knew anyone in the library; staff were hidden away, uninvolved with the rest of the campus. This external perception contrasted sharply with the librarians' self-image. In our opinion, we were innovative, provided excellent service, and offered a strong collection. Librarians actively participated in campus committees, as well as the broader professional library community. Whether the services had become invisible because they were taken for granted, or whether we were deceiving ourselves (Wolpert 1998), it is difficult to say. Since the negative feedback was so pervasive, the University Librarian decided to address these gaps in library user satisfaction by improving campus awareness of the benefits of library resources and services, raising our profile, and promoting the high quality library collection.

LAUNCHING THE PROMOTIONAL CAMPAIGN

The timing of the decision to pursue a promotional campaign could not have been better. With a new and visionary University Librarian at the helm, we had recently implemented a new Integrated Library System (ILS), opened an Education Resources Centre (in support of education programs), relocated and expanded the Archives and Special Collections, redesigned the library web pages, and improved service hours. Several additional projects, such as a comprehensive evaluation of the collection, the management and integration of E-resources, and preparing for a medical program, were in the early planning stages. In other words, there were numerous accomplishments to share with the rest of the institution.

In November 2002, the University Librarian charged the authors with developing a series of multi-faceted promotional activities based on the American Library Association's (ALA) "@ your library" framework. We were to consult with the University Communications Department (responsible for marketing and promotion of UNBC) as necessary, and to be as creative and as cost-effective as possible. Cost-effectiveness was key since a budget had not been established for such initiatives; however, approximately $1,250 was allocated from the library supply budget to begin the campaign. Interaction with the Communications staff allowed us to tap into their public relations expertise, a large collection of university photographs, and pricing and contact information for promotional products, such as pens, posters, and display panels.

UNBC's promotional materials are visually attractive, focus on the people at the university, and make extensive use of the university colours of green and gold. They also reflect the beauty of BC's northern environment and the institution's mandate to serve the northern regions of the province. These promotional items convey the vitality of a young but rapidly developing university. We determined that the library's promotional materials should have a similar tone and should, wherever possible, emulate the themes, elements, and colours of the institution's promotional pieces. In doing so, the library would be identified as an integral part of the university, while at the same time highlighting the services and resources specific to the library.

Our brainstorming sessions produced ideas for posters and a display panel centered on the themes of research, accessibility, library resources, services, and collections. Using the "@ your library" framework as a branding mechanism, catch phrases were created that established the distinctive quality desired in the promotional material. Catch phrases included: "possibilities @ your library," "exploring @ your library," and "at home @ your library." The phrase "research @ your fingertips," a variation on "@ your library," became a consistent slogan to build brand identity. "Research @ your fingertips" (especially when linked to relevant text and photos) suggests an academic focus with an emphasis on technology, innovation, and accessibility that one would expect of a research library.

As our ideas expanded, we refined the principles and strategies of our marketing approach. The principles included: (a) establish specific goals for promotion; (b) use a variety of media avenues to spread our message(s); (c) promote within the library; (d) promote outside of the library; (e) inform others about librarians' professional and/or scholarly accomplishments; (f) use positive images to convey our message(s); (g) recognize that marketing is ongoing; and (h) evaluate and revise to keep the message(s) from becoming stale. With these goals in mind, we carried out a variety of strategies to raise awareness about the library, to promote new initiatives, and to convey the library's message of innovative service.

PROMOTIONAL STRATEGIES

Display Panel

Although several departments throughout the university use portable display units at promotional events both on- and off-campus, the library had not previously participated in these organized events and did not possess a display unit. Indeed, communication with the library about such events had been inconsistent to poor, contributing to misperceptions about the library. We weren't invited to attend because we had not expressed an interest, but we could not express an interest because we were not aware of the opportunity. People did not think to approach us because of the perception that we "kept to ourselves," and organizers of such events were perhaps uncertain of who to contact at the Weller Library. This lesson was added to our list of guiding principles and marketing strategies: express an interest to be involved, explore opportunities, and ensure that event organizers have contact names.

Because of our recently established rapport with Communications personnel, we learned about a planned event, UNBC Day, which was to take place in January 2003. With this deadline in mind, one of the first projects was to purchase a portable tabletop display unit. (See Figure 1.) The unit frame is designed for three double-sided panels forming a triptych. Text and the photos are affixed to the panels; the panels slide into the frame which conveniently folds flat for transport. The ability to interchange the panels to suit the purpose of the event lends additional flexibility. Updating the display text and photos on new panels would be coordinated through the Communications Department.

It was important to create a display that could be used for a variety of promotional purposes and would not become dated too quickly. To this end, we selected bold, vibrant photographs that would catch the eye

FIGURE 1. Portable Tabletop Display

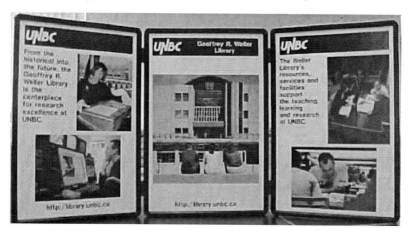

from a distance as well as focus on the services we wanted to promote. Because of the rich stock of photos stored at the Communications Department, selection of appropriate photos was very easy. The overall message was innovation, state of the art technology, a rich variety of resources, and a comfortable, welcoming environment. With the library name featured prominently across the top of the middle panel, succinct information was interspersed with attractive and relevant photos on the panels. In determining the design layout, care was taken to avoid confusing clutter. Instead, operating from the premise that "less is more," we consciously created a display with the text and photos arranged in a way that emulates the natural eye movement, that is, left to right and downward. When using the display, additional materials are generally arranged on the table in front of it. Depending on the event, these might include a selection of monographs, journals, promotional pens, balloons, or a laptop showing the library web pages.

The Weller Library can now participate with professionalism and pride in university-sponsored events. Further, the display makes it possible for us to leave the library and reach out to clients and potential clients, rather than expecting them to seek us out. The university community has appreciated the library presence and feedback has been positive. This project was cost-effective, (the total cost was $250), flexible, easy to create, and certainly has contributed to building brand identity for the library.

Posters

We next turned our attention to the creation of posters with the idea of spreading a message more broadly than was possible with a portable tabletop display. Drawing again on the expertise of the Communications Department, we worked with their 10 × 17 inch poster template.

We determined that the three key messages to convey were: (a) the ability to access the library remotely; (b) the rich variety of resources available in the library; and (c) the library's technological innovation. These themes were selected because they would address a general lack of awareness on campus of these resources and services. Creating three separate posters to convey the messages, we believed, would help spread awareness more effectively. One poster might be overlooked, but three that were similar, yet distinct from each other would catch attention, reinforce the message, and raise library visibility.

During the development phase, we brainstormed by sketching out on paper the concept, visual images, and wording in support of each theme.

Catch phrases, mentioned above, built around "@ your library" were printed along the top of each poster. For example, the catch phrase used for the poster promoting remote access is "at home @ your library." (See Figure 2.) The wording on each poster is brief and can be read at a glance. The text along the bottom of the three posters is the same: the slogan "research @ your fingertips" with the full name of the Geoffrey R. Weller Library and the UNBC logo in order to be consistent in building brand identity. Care was taken to create a clean, uncluttered display with text, colour, and photo balanced for natural eye movement.

We described our "vision" to the Communications staff whose photos taken for this purpose beautifully captured the concepts and featured students in the relevant settings. As is evident in Figure 2, the photo in this poster depicts a young woman, clearly in a comfortable environment, who is able to access the library resources without barriers. An interesting point about the photos is that the individuals featured are not smiling at the viewer, but instead appear to be completely absorbed in what they are doing. This, we believe, makes the photos seem more natural and less "posed," thereby lending an authentic quality to the posters and the message. Further, the photos are fresh and glowing with "youthful vitality," and, as with the display unit, they will not become quickly

FIGURE 2. "Research @ your fingertips" Promotional Poster

dated. The poster template lends itself to easy modification of the message, photo, and colours so that updating this promotional tool to keep it fresh is always an option.

The layouts were completed by the graphic artist of the Communications Department and were printed by a local print shop. We ordered 100 copies of each poster for a total cost of $300, which proved to be excellent value.

The posters are displayed strategically throughout the library, at its entrance, around campus, the residences, and were sent to UNBC's four satellite campuses. In addition, we hand-delivered copies to a few key people in the university administration as a method of communicating the promotional campaign.

The posters have been well-received, with many positive comments. In fact, staff members from other departments have expressed a desire to develop a similar series to promote their own services and resources. The posters have also been popular with the students, so much so that one poster in particular is regularly stolen from its display spot by the library entrance.

Promotional Giveaways

Handing out small promotional "treats" in the library, at events, or to enhance a display, was very appealing. Distinctive red plastic ALA "@" bookmarks were purchased through the Ontario Library Association (OLA), the Canadian distributor for ALA @ promotional materials, for a cost of $200 for 500 bookmarks. A local print store provided inexpensive pens, (500 at $1 each), with the message:

UNBC Weller Library
research @ your fingertips

Both of these items were kept at the Circulation Desk and were handed out at the beginning of the September term as part of the "Welcome Week" orientation program. At the same time, an announcement was sent to the student newspaper, *Over the Edge*, which announced library hours for the fall term and urged students to come in for their free pen and bookmark. The idea behind this was to attract the students to the library early in the term, as opposed to having them discover the library just before their assignments were due. The pens were also given away at meetings and conferences attended by UNBC librarians. The pens were extremely popular and we ran out of them quickly, but the bookmarks did not seem to be as desirable. We will most likely continue to purchase the pens but not the bookmarks.

Exhibits

Regular exhibits organized around library-related themes or complementing university events was another successful marketing initiative. The main entrance of the library is graced with a wide glass panel between two glass doors. Several feet from the doors on the left is the Circulation counter; further in and on the right is the Reference Desk. Because the entrance has open visibility with good sight lines, the space immediately in front of the middle glass panel lends itself beautifully to exhibits. A glass display cabinet (18 × 36 × 73 inches) relocated to this spot did not spoil the design features of the entrance and allowed people on either side of the glass entrance to appreciate the exhibits.

The first exhibit, for Canada's "Freedom to Read Week," included books that had been banned at some point in history. Each book was accompanied by a small card giving the title of the book and a brief explanation for the banning. A selection of quotations regarding censorship from well-known individuals, such as Salman Rushdie, was also included, along with "Freedom to Read" posters from the Canadian Library Association (CLA). Since then, exhibit themes have included: Media Democracy Day, Canada Book Week featuring local authors, a celebration of Dr. Seuss' 100th birthday, Remembrance Day, and a Welcome to new and returning students in September and January. The exhibit changes about once a month.

As with the other promotional strategies, we consciously aimed for an academic touch in creating the exhibits. With an extremely small budget for material, this sometimes posed a challenge. However, with our "less is more" philosophy, as well as a very talented library assistant, we have been able to successfully balance professional content with artistic flair. The exhibits have received many compliments and patrons are often observed clustered around the cabinet discussing the topics. For the low cost per exhibit ($5-$20), they have provided tremendous PR value and, based on the positive feedback from faculty, staff, and students, the impact has been significant in terms of increasing library awareness.

University Publications

With the goal of reaching a broad audience, we took advantage of two existing university bi-weekly publications: the *Bulletin*, a newsletter published by the Communications Department to inform faculty and staff of university activities, and the student newspaper, *Over the Edge*. Library information is included free of charge and circulated directly to our target market of the faculty, staff, and students of UNBC.

Communiqués to the *Bulletin* included announcements of the professional and/or scholarly accomplishments of librarians, along with significant developments in library resources that would be of interest to the faculty. Because the information presented in this newsletter is very readable and can be quickly absorbed, we know that readership is high. As a result, it has proven to be an excellent vehicle for getting key information out to the faculty.

The editor of the student newspaper was more than willing to accommodate our proposal of regular submissions from the library. A standard 5 × 6 inch template was created with a photo of the library, the header *Did you know?* and the *"Research @ your fingertips"* slogan as the footer. (See Figure 3.) The centre was used to communicate general information (library hours during exams), current events (new resources, displays), or to highlight services (ILL, Distance Services) of interest to students. The submissions were written well ahead of time and submitted in accordance with publication deadlines.

FUTURE DIRECTIONS

Having delivered a variety of organized promotional strategies for over a year, we have received positive comments and compliments on the more successful approaches. The tabletop display, the posters, library exhibits, and the pens are cost-effective and offer excellent PR value. Submitting information to the *Bulletin* has also been a good strategy, but we are less certain (due to a lack of feedback) that the students are reading the information submitted to the student newspaper. However, since there is no cost and it is easy to create informational blurbs for this media source, we will likely continue to promote the library through this avenue. Exploiting the familiar "@" symbol has given us tremendous flexibility in developing catch phrases that promote library resources and services. The "@ your library" framework has proven to

FIGURE 3. Library Submission to Student Newspaper

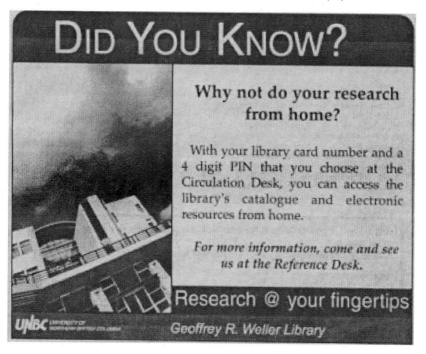

be an excellent PR tool, serving to raise the library's profile and build brand identity. We will continue with these approaches, refine the strategies that work, and brainstorm for new ideas. However, there are additional and more formal processes which should be implemented to strengthen promotional activities. Specifically, three areas have been identified: a budget allocation to carry out promotional strategies, methods to measure outcomes, and a formal marketing plan document.

In order to continue with the promotional campaign, it is clear that a budget is required. The literature certainly supports this and Wolpert (1998), for example, notes that libraries need to become more sophisticated in their promotional activities. In any organization, a single department's promotional materials and activities are competing with hundreds of other glossy literature and flashy promotions that are eye-catching and appealing. It is a challenge to create materials that will not be overlooked in this vast array of colour and glitz. Since the University Librarian (in consultation with the librarians) has determined that it is a priority to promote the Geoffrey R. Weller Library, to do so effectively requires that library materials be of a professional quality. To this end, we have recommended to the University Librarian that an annual budget of $1,000 be allocated to support promotional activities.

Because the results of promotional practices are often intangible, measuring outcomes can be difficult. To date, we have assessed results based only on informal feedback from patrons, more formal comments made at meetings (which have been recorded in the minutes), and general user reactions to the strategies (such as enthusiastic reaction to the pens, the posters, and the discussions around the display case). Based on the anecdotal evidence collected, we are cautiously optimistic that a positive change towards the library has occurred. However, we are particularly interested in whether or not people have become more aware of library resources and if there have been significant changes in perceptional attitudes of the library. As we move forward with promotional plans for the Weller Library, it would be helpful to measure the effectiveness of the PR initiatives through a more formal assessment, possibly with focus groups or surveys.

The next important phase will be writing a comprehensive marketing plan. Although we developed a set of guiding principles as noted above, a formal marketing plan would be broader than just promotional strategies. The document will outline marketing goals, principles and practices, in addition to setting directions. The plan will include methods by which outcomes can be measured in order to evaluate the success of the promotional strategies. Further, this document will be an evolving plan, regularly reviewed and updated to mirror new directions being taken by the library. Ideally, a formal marketing plan should be integrated with the library's strategic plan, and would therefore be instrumental in goal-setting, budget planning, and overall strategic planning for the library.

While it is important that the library's marketing plan become part of the strategic plan, the document should also reflect institutional goals. In the past year, UNBC has finalized an institution-wide *Action Plan* (strategic plan) to which, understandably, much significance has been attached. Including relevant components from the *Action Plan* into Weller Library's marketing plan will strengthen library credibility within the institution.

IMPLICATIONS FOR PRACTICE

The literature analyzing promotion of the academic library presents strong arguments that marketing is critical, due to rapid expansion of new technologies, the complexities of information storage and retrieval, and tremendous financial pressures (Murphy 1991; Denham 1995; Dodsworth 1998; Wolpert 1998; Harrington and Li 2001). It is interesting that, despite strong arguments in the literature advocating marketing and marketing plans in academic libraries, there are relatively few articles written on this topic. This poses several questions: are academic librarians turning to the marketing literature of other disciplines for guidance?; have librarians taken the literature seriously and implemented marketing strategies?; just how much marketing is taking place in academic libraries?; and the most important questions: has it been successful and has it made a difference?

In terms of "to market or not to market," complacency is not an option. The risks of being reticent about marketing are too great: a poor image, false perceptions, lack of support and advocacy, and missed opportunities in the big institutional picture. Marketing can and does serve many purposes. Not only can it be instrumental in raising the profile of the academic library, but marketing also serves to educate and inform users about the important research function the library provides. Librarians are only too aware that most individuals do not understand the complexities of library resources and services and that too many students do not recognize the link between using the library and academic success. Murphy (1991) notes that everything an organization does should revolve around an understanding of customer need. Librarians recognize that, in general, patrons may not understand what library resources and services they require and therefore may not know how to ask for help. It is up to us to anticipate user needs, encourage users to ask for help, and inform users clearly of library resources. Carrying out strong marketing initiatives to accomplish this can greatly enhance user awareness. If we do not communicate clearly, often, and in a highly organized fashion about who we are, what we do, and why they need us, who else will do that for us?

CONCLUSION

Promotional strategies do not have to be complicated or expensive to be successful. Often, the most successful strategies are cost-effective and still achieve significant PR value. However, cost-effective does not mean cheap or poorly executed. A high standard of professional quality should be evident in the message(s) and image(s).

A well-organized marketing campaign must be based on strong guiding principles and reflect institutional goals. When academic librarians are developing marketing and promotional strategies, it is important to include basic PR practices such as ongoing communication, looking for opportunities to promote the library, and expressing an interest in participating in institutional activities.

In this challenging environment where academic institutions are being asked to justify activities, budgets, and resources, marketing and promotion take on greater importance than they have in the past. When this is added to the perennial image problems suffered by libraries and librarians, it is more than time to implement strong promotional practices. Academic librarians cannot afford the luxury of assuming that everyone will recognize their significant role within the institution. Successful PR campaigns improve the library's image, leading to increased advocacy for the library, and can win support around significant issues such as institutional budget allocations. As noted in the literature and through practical experience, the positive links between improved marketing and support for the library are inarguably clear.

QUICK BIB

Dodsworth, E. 1998. Marketing academic libraries: A necessary plan. *The Journal of Academic Librarianship.* 24(4): 320-22.

Murphy, K. 1991. Marketing and library management. *Library Administration & Management.* 5(3): 155-58.

Wolpert, A. 1998. Services to remote users: Marketing the library's role. *Library Trends.* 47(1): 21-42.

REFERENCES

Black, N. E. 2001. Emerging technologies: Tools for distance education and library services. *Journal of Library Administration.* 31(3/4): 45-59.

Brewerton, A. 2003. Inspired! Award-winning library marketing. *New Library World.* 104(7/8): 267-78.

Brunsdale, M. 2000. From mild to wild: Strategies for promoting academic libraries to undergraduates. *Reference & User Services Quarterly.* 39(4): 331-36.

Denham, R. 1995. Strategic planning: Creating the future. *Feliciter* 41: 38-43.

Dodsworth, E. 1998. Marketing academic libraries: A necessary plan. *The Journal of Academic Librarianship.* 24(4): 320-22.

Harrington, D. L., and X. Li. 2001. Spinning an academic web community: Measuring marketing effectiveness. *Journal of Academic Librarianship.* 27(3): 199-208.

Murphy, K. 1991. Marketing and library management. *Library Administration & Management.* 5(3): 155-58.

Rankings 2004. Primarily undergraduate. *Macleans.* http://www.macleans.ca/universities Retrieved March 24, 2005.

Spencer, D. B. 2002. Boosting libraries at university orientations. *College & Research Libraries News.* 63(6): 418-20.

Wolpert, A. 1998. Services to remote users: Marketing the library's role. *Library Trends.* 47(1): 21-42.

Getting the Word Out:
Publicizing Library Programs and Services
to the Community

Rob Withers

SUMMARY. Although the primary constituencies of academic libraries are their faculty, students, and staff, the programs and displays that they and their Friends organizations sponsor may be of interest to the surrounding community. Effectively reaching these groups requires a concerted effort. Information must be written for an external audience, and contact information for all prospective news providers must be ready to use. Libraries may also avail themselves of low-cost or no-cost methods for disseminating information. By reaching out to community members, college and university libraries will encourage local residents to take advantage of the programming and services offered by the library and may influence them to become more closely tied to their institution. *[Article copies available for a fee from The Haworth Document Delivery Service: 1-800-HAWORTH. E-mail address: <docdelivery@haworthpress.com> Website: <http://www.HaworthPress.com> © 2005 by The Haworth Press, Inc. All rights reserved.]*

Rob Withers (BA, College of Wooster; MA, University of North Carolina; MLS, North Carolina Central University) is Assistant to the Dean and University Librarian, King Library, Miami University, Oxford, OH 45056 (address e-mail to: rwithers@lib.muohio.edu).

[Haworth co-indexing entry note]: "Getting the Word Out: Publicizing Library Programs and Services to the Community." Withers, Rob. Co-published simultaneously in *College & Undergraduate Libraries* (The Haworth Information Press, an imprint of The Haworth Press, Inc.) Vol. 12, No. 1/2, 2005, pp. 35-45; and: *Real-Life Marketing and Promotion Strategies in College Libraries: Connecting with Campus and Community* (ed: Barbara Whitney Petruzzelli) The Haworth Information Press, an imprint of The Haworth Press, Inc., 2005, pp. 35-45. Single or multiple copies of this article are available for a fee from The Haworth Document Delivery Service [1-800-HAWORTH, 9:00 a.m. - 5:00 p.m. (EST). E-mail address: docdelivery@haworthpress.com].

doi:10.1300/J106v12n01_03

KEYWORDS. Public relations, community outreach, library programming, academic libraries

Academic libraries have many audiences with which they need to communicate. Effective communication with faculty, staff, and students through on-campus mechanisms may promote use of new resources and services, enhance attendance at library-sponsored events, and encourage on-campus support for library programs. However, the exhibits, programs, and services that academic libraries and their Friends organizations sponsor may also be of interest to the surrounding community. Placing information in off-campus media targets community members who may be advocates for libraries and library funding (Spalding 2003, 159).

Effectively reaching these groups requires a concerted effort, but is essential in these challenging budgetary times. In an overview of public relations, Charlotte Dugan observes that academic libraries may mistakenly assume that there is little need for outreach because they believe that they have a captive audience within the academic community, or that their funding is secure (Dugan 1994, 11). Programs and exhibits help to draw people into the library building and acquaint them with the full range of library services (Fink 2001, 40). By attracting community members into the library for these events, outreach to the community has the potential to strengthen direct and indirect support for the library by actively interesting these people in its welfare–provided that libraries maximize the opportunities for such exposure.

RECRUIT PROMINENT INDIVIDUALS FOR PROGRAMS AND EXHIBITS

The participation of well-known alumni or community members in library programs and activities can be a major attraction for off-campus individuals. At the author's institution, the African-American Read-In has engaged well-known figures from nearby Cincinnati as keynote speakers, including the new superintendent of the Cincinnati Public Schools and members of the Tuskegee Airmen. In some cases, a library staff member may have prior personal contact with the individual; but often, the speaker is recruited by explaining the event and the expectations for their involvement (e.g., a 15-30 minute talk, as well as lunch).

High-profile individuals also attract news coverage because they are well-known to the press.

EXPLOIT AVAILABLE NO COST/LOW COST ADVERTISING

Publicity need not entail a hefty advertising budget. Low-cost options include announcements that run in between scheduled programming on public access cable television channels, public service announcements on non-commercial radio stations (Sass 2002), and community calendars which are often sponsored by chambers of commerce, radio and TV stations, or local governments. These options involve little expense other than the staff time needed to review deadlines and requirements and to submit information, and are likely to reach a broad audience.

Establishing an electronic mailing list can also disseminate information about library programming to interested parties (Natarajan 2002, 27; Dodsworth 1998, 321). This list can be developed by asking participants at library programs or at alumni events in which the libraries participate to contribute their e-mail addresses. E-mail lists have the advantage of not incurring the printing and postage expenses that traditional mailed announcements and newsletters require. To mitigate concern about spam, it may be advisable to stipulate the maximum number of e-mails to be sent over a given time period (e.g., no more than once per month). Diligently seeking out people who express an interest in the library's programs, particularly those who attend, helps to build a core group of regular participants.

Creating print-based publicity such as flyers, postcards, or table tents can entail more expense than options described above, but costs may be manageable if paper costs are conserved. Miami University Libraries print smaller-format, "four-to-a-page" flyers that have proven successful. (See Figure 1.)

The effectiveness of this type of publicity can be boosted if items are distributed in places likely to attract people who might have an interest in library-sponsored events. Bookstores and public libraries are ideal places for posting such news, but flyers hung in K-12 schools, grocery stores, medical clinics, and retirement homes also have the advantage of reaching large numbers of people with a relatively limited number of printed advertisements.

Some locations have requirements that must be met before flyers or other items are displayed. Restrictions may include how far in advance of events they can be posted, how long they will be displayed, or what

FIGURE 1. Four-to-a-Page Flyer

African-Americans at Miami
A digital collection in celebration of
African-American History Month

African Americans have enriched our country and our campus. During African-American history month, take time to learn about African-American's contributions to Miami.

- Which nationally known African-American leader spoke at Miami in 1959— and where can you find a recording of his speech?

- The first African-American student to live on campus arrived over 41 years after the first African-American student graduated from Miami. Who were these students and when did they arrive?

Find out! Learn about the achievements of all of these individuals!
Visit the University Libraries' "African-Americans at Miami" Digital Collection:

http://www.lib.muohio.edu/afamhist

kinds of events they will publicize. Rather than haphazardly posting announcements that may be refused or removed, compile a list of venues and gather information that includes a contact person, turnaround time for approving announcements, time limits, and types of events that may be publicized.

Other sources of low-cost advertising may include table tents for area restaurants, booths at community events, or signs on busses or on benches at bus stops. While still relatively low cost, these types of advertising will require money. To maximize use of these resources, contact local printers to establish costs and time needed for printing. In the case of advertising on busses or bus stop benches, contact transit agencies ahead of time to obtain information about advertising rates, duration of advertising, advance time needed to secure advertising, and any guidelines about content.

Producing and distributing flyers may require little more than staff time and access to a color printer. The more visually attractive these items are, the better, but remember: people will base their decision to attend a program or use a service more on the content of the announcement than the graphic design. Provided you have identified appropriate locations for distributing information, a little leg work or a small amount of postage may be all that is needed to alert the surrounding community to library programming.

GET THE MOST "BANG FOR YOUR BUCK" WITH PROMOTIONAL ITEMS

Many promotional items contain little more than a name, URL, or slogan. However, libraries benefit from items which enable them to communicate a greater amount of information and to spread multiple messages over an extended period of time. Mouse pads can provide one option for accomplishing this goal. At Miami University Libraries, mouse pads which accommodated inserts were distributed to faculty. Afterward, the faculty periodically received new inserts with information about various library services (Moeckel 2000, 273). A similar model might be used to distribute information to frequent library users or to regular attendees of library-sponsored events. Mouse pads have the advantage of being able to communicate substantive quantities of information, compared to pens, notepads, and the like. However, they also cost significantly more than such items. Soft shell mouse pads can cost up to 3-4 times as much per item, and hard shell mouse pads can cost 4-6 times as much. And unless prepared to pay for mailing expenses, libraries must consider how they will effectively distribute these items to large quantities of people.

Another model for delivering messages over an extended period of time to both on- and off-campus audiences might be a calendar featuring library events throughout the year. It could even include ordering information for the following year's library calendar.

With all promotional items, be wary of high-cost for items that convey little information. When distributing pens, pencils, magnets, notepads, etc., that have limited space for text, use the space wisely. Don't stop with the library name, but add a URL, phone number, or library hours, if possible. In doing so, you make it possible for the recipient to seek out the library.

COMMUNICATE EFFECTIVELY WITH THE NEWS MEDIA

Newspapers, radio stations, and television stations can all help to disseminate news of important library purchases or programs open to the public. Press releases should be issued well in advance of the event you wish to publicize, so that editors can find a time when space is available for your story. Releases should include contact information for someone who can answer questions, as well as basic information such as time, place, cost, and intended audiences. Be sure to mention that the public is welcome.

Maximizing coverage of library events requires more, however, than a blanket press release distributed to various news outlets. Larger media organizations often have more than one reporter or editor who might be interested in news about library events and services. Information not addressed to a specific person or office may not reach the person most interested in the story, or may encounter delays in reaching that individual, reducing chances of receiving timely publicity. Whenever possible, send releases to specific reporters or editors. These might include reporters who cover the geographical area in which the library is located, edit columns about the arts, edit or write education reports, write stories on information technology, or compile events calendars.

Public information offices at a library's institution should always receive copies of any press releases to be distributed to the news media so that they are prepared to respond to questions that might arise. Some public information offices prefer to distribute, and in many cases even write, all press releases for a campus. Check with them to find out their preferred approach.

If the library writes the press release, ask the public information staff to review it ahead of time, so they can provide helpful suggestions on where to submit the press release or how to revise it. If the public information office writes the release, ask to see a draft and feel free to suggest changes that might help tailor your release to off-campus audiences or to the audiences of specific publications.

Public information offices may be less interested in adding listings to community calendars or to one-sentence summaries of educational or cultural programming found in many daily and weekly newspapers. Know the policies and preferences of your public information office before disseminating information.

COMPILE MEDIA INFORMATION AHEAD OF TIME

Trying to acquire media contact information and submission instructions for newspapers, public access television channels, and other advertising venues is a time-consuming process. Trying to do this on the spur of the moment can lead to error. To be ready to access this information whenever needed, libraries should compile contact information in advance. Identify the media outlets which might disseminate information about library programs and services, and then contact the organization to find out the best contact person(s) for library events. Keep a record of names, addresses, phone numbers, and deadlines for submitting information. (See Figure 2.)

To keep the contact information chart as accurate as possible, plan to review and update it once per semester. If there are reporters who frequently report on information about the library, consider an occasional thank you note or small gifts, such as a commemorative library item, to recognize their efforts and maintain a working relationship.

TAILOR COMMUNICATIONS
TO A COMMUNITY AUDIENCE

Information follows the path of least resistance–it is more likely to be published if it requires minimal editing. Any information that will ap-

FIGURE 2. Media Contact Information Chart

	Media Outlet	Department/Column	Deadline	Conact Name	Contact E-mail/Phone
Newspapers		Happenings		Jim Knippenberg	jknippenberg@enquirer.com
		Neighborhoods		Randy McNutt	rmcnutt@enquirer.com
		Religion		Rachel Thompson	rthompson@enquirer.com
	Cincinnati Enquirer	What's Happening	2 weeks prior	Jason Nebel	312 Elm St/Cinti, OH 45202
	Cincinnati Post	Enterntianment		Rick Bird	rbird@cincypost.com
	CityBeat		Thursday before	Brandon Brady	bbrady@citybeat.com
		Butler County Bureau		Jessica Brown	jebrown@coxohio.com
		Community		Peggy McCracken	pmccracken@coxohio.com
		Advertisements		Kay Knox	KKnox@coxohio.com
	Hamilton Journal-News	Enterntianment		Rick Jones	RJones@coxohio.com
	Oxford Press	Community		Ben Poston	bposton@coxohio.com
	Miami Report	Editor	Friday before	Beth Weaver	weaverpg@muohio.edu
	Miami Student	News			news@mustudent.muohio.edu
Events Calendar	WMUB	Community Calendar			http://events.publicbroadcasting.
	WMOH	News Director		Steve Vaughan	stevevaughn@wmoh.com
	WAKW Events Line				513-956-WAKW.
	Dayton Daily News	Events Calendar			http://www.activedayton.com/sh
	Hamilton Chamber of	Events Calendar			http://www.activedayton.com/sh
	WDTN	Events Calendar			buchbeat@wdtn.com
	WHIO	Events Calendar			http://www.activedayton.com/sh
Television Stations	WKRC	send message			http://wkrc.com/logic/index.php?
	WCPO	report a story			http://wcpo.com/news/tips.html
	WCPO	Public service announcemen	4 weeks before		500 Central Ave. Cincinnati, OH
	WLWT	News Tips			http://www.wlwt.com/news/news
	WLWT	News Tips			cinnews@channelcincinnati.com

pear in off-campus publications or locations must be written from a non-campus-centric perspective. Community members will need to know more about parking restrictions and meeting locations, for example, than an on-campus audience would. Jargon should be explained or avoided altogether. A tailored message serves the audience best and makes them more likely to attend programming and use library services.

Many community calendars require specific types of information provided in a specific order. When submitting to an events calendar, make sure that your submission meets these content and format requirements.

At best, submitting press releases or calendar listings which are incomplete or require editing will delay publication of the submission. At worst, the editors may decide not to include it at all.

PREPARE FOR POSSIBLE FOLLOW-UP

Press releases and flyers should always include names of individuals who can provide further information if needed. This makes it easy for reporters to verify information or obtain quotes to add to a story. Also, consider whether public information officers or other on-campus units outside the library might be contacted about press releases that the library issues. If so, be sure that these people are aware of the event or service you're publicizing, so that they can respond to any questions that might be directed to them.

Finally, don't forget the important promotional role played by librarians and library staff. Make sure that they are fully informed about events and services being publicized to the community. Since they are in the front line of interacting with patrons in person and on the telephone, they need to be able to answer questions and to know the people to whom they can refer requests for more information (Wallace 2002).

PUBLICIZE AFTER-THE-FACT

Photograph all library events. Newspapers, particularly those which emphasize local or neighborhood coverage, often print photographs with brief captions to take up space on slow news days, and a few may even devote an entire page to pictures from community events. Photographs of speakers or honorees may be welcome. Though no longer concerned with promoting attendance at the pictured events, the library still benefits from this publicity. The photographs raise the visibility of the library and portray it as a dynamic place. Readers may be more interested in attending future events as a result.

Not all photographs are effective in newspapers. For example, a photograph of people browsing through books at a book sale is less likely to see print than a photograph of a well-known individual or a group of enthusiastic shoppers loaded down with boxes or bags of books. Particularly in local newspapers, emphasize faces; editors are interested in showing familiar faces to the community (Shepard 2004).

Photographs submitted to the newspaper should be accompanied by a document providing information about the event and the individual pictured. Because the space available for photographs and their captions may vary, include both a short, one- or two-sentence description and a longer, one- or two-paragraph description. This eliminates the need for someone to edit text which may be too long or too short for the available space.

REVIEW OTHER LIBRARIES' PUBLICITY

Not sure about what kinds of information the library should disseminate? Read local daily and weekly newspapers regularly, view an entire cycle of announcements on public access television channels, and look around for other library publicity. These can provide a guide for the kinds of information that can be distributed, and the place(s) in which it should appear.

Reviewing media in this way can also provide a benchmark for the library's efforts to publicize events and services. Take a look around your community to see if any program announcements readily catch your eye. Gather and review promotional materials from other libraries and see how wording, placement of information, and use of graphics may hinder or enhance the effectiveness of the communication. Survey listings of community events and news coverage to see when and where other libraries appear. Compare the coverage of programming and services at your library to others that provide similar types and numbers of programs. If your library is receiving disproportionately less coverage, critique your existing efforts and brainstorm ways to make your library more visible.

CONCLUSION

Academic libraries provide services, resources, and programming that can be of great value to the communities in which they are located. To make sure that community members know about and are encouraged to take advantage of the library resources that interest them, academic libraries need to identify methods for publicizing their resources which are effective, but which do not adversely strain library budgets. Publicizing events and services through news providers and low-cost advertising can be very effective. Provided you have done your homework about where and how to distribute information ahead of time, disseminating library news can be done with a minimal investment of money and staff time. At the author's institution, aggressive, yet low-cost, publicity has increased the diversity of audiences at library programs.

At the very least, publicity aims to attract more people to library programs and to make its services and resources more visible. And by involving community members in the library and the campus, libraries may influence someone who might someday donate books, contribute money, or even decide to attend their institution.

QUICK BIB

Ashcroft, L.S. 1994. "Effective Press Releases." *Library Management* 15(8): 24-27.

Baverstock, Alison. 2002. *Publicity, Newsletters and Press Releases*. Oxford: Oxford University Press.

Craumer, Martha. 2002. "Why Your Press Releases Aren't Making News." Harvard Management Communication Letter 5(1): 3.

Shepard, Michael T. [n.d.] "Attracting Readers Through Effective Design." Quoted in *Teaching Tips*. http://www.highschooljournalism.org/teachers/tipsattracting6.htm.

REFERENCES

Ashcroft, L.S. 1994. "Effective Press Releases." *Library Management* 15(8): 24-27.

Baverstock, Alison. 2002. *Publicity, Newsletters and Press Releases*. Oxford: Oxford University Press.

Craumer, Martha. 2002. "Why Your Press Releases Aren't Making News." *Harvard Management Communication Letter* 5(1): 3.

Dodsworth, Ellen M. 1998. "Marketing Academic Libraries: A Necessary Plan." *The Journal of Academic Librarianship* 24(4): 320-2.

Dugan, Charlotte A. 1994. "Virtually Possible: Academic Library Public Relations." *Technicalities* 14: 10-12.

Fink, Deborah and Bonnie McCune. 2001. "Marketing Libraries." *Colorado Libraries* 27(4): 5-40.

LeBeau, Chris. 1999. "Marketing Basics in a Changing Information Age." *Nebraska Library Association Quarterly* 30(4): 3-11.

Moeckel, Nancy and Joanne M. Goode. 2000. "Building a Better Mousetrap: Using a Mousepad to Publicize Products and Services to Faculty." *College & Research Libraries News* 61(4): 273-5.

McCoombs, Gillian M. 2002. "A Case Study of Successful Library Fund-Raising: The Right Mix of Deliberate Strategy, 'Opportunity Knocks,' and 'Lady Luck.'" *The Bottom Line: Managing Library Finances* 15(3): 110-115.

Natarajan, M. 2002. "E-mail as a Marketing Tool for Information Products and Services." *DESIDOC Bulletin of Information Technology* 22(3): 27-34.

Orava, Hilkka. 1997. "Marketing is an Attitude of Mind." 63rd IFLA General Conference–Conference Program and Proceedings (August 31-September 5, 1997). http://www.ifla.org/IV/ifla63/63orah.htm.

Sass, Rivkah K. 2002. "Marketing the Worth of the Library." *Library Journal* 127(11): 37-38.

Shepard, Michael T. [n.d.] "Attracting Readers Through Effective Design." Quoted in *Teaching Tips.* http://www.highschooljournalism.org/teachers/tipsattracting6.htm.

Spalding, Helen K. 2003. "It's Not Just Academic @ Your Library." *College & Research Libraries News* 64(3): 159-160.

Wallace, Linda and Peggy Barber. 2002. "Ten Marketing Ideas and Tips for Virtual Reference Service." American Library Association Conference (June 15, 2002). http://www.ssdesign.com/librarypr/content/p070802a.shtml.

Matching Media to Audience Equals Marketing Success

Kathleen Conley
Toni Tucker

SUMMARY. Academic libraries tend to differentiate the medium of their marketing messages but not the messages themselves. Of paramount importance is the identification and description of the library's target audiences and the selection of media most likely to generate a positive response to the library and increase use of its resources.

This article identifies target audiences desirable for undergraduate academic libraries and describes how to develop mutually beneficial relationships with these audiences. The positive impact that results from audience and media segmentation in the areas of library funding, awareness, use, and attitude are noted. Examples are given from successful public relations initiatives at Milner Library at Illinois State University. *[Article copies available for a fee from The Haworth Document Delivery Service: 1-800-HAWORTH. E-mail address: <docdelivery@haworthpress.com> Website: <http://www.HaworthPress.com> © 2005 by The Haworth Press, Inc. All rights reserved.]*

Kathleen Conley (MLS, University of Illinois, Urbana-Champaign; MA in English Literature, Illinois State University) is Head, General Reference and Documents, Milner Library, Illinois State University, Campus Box 8900, Normal, IL 61790-8900 (address e-mail to: kcconle@ilstu.edu).

Toni Tucker (MLIS, Dominican University; MS in Education, Purdue University) is Assistant to the Dean for Grants, Development and Public Relations, Milner Library, Illinois State University, Campus Box 8900, Normal, IL 61790-8900 (address e-mail to: ttucker@ilstu.edu).

[Haworth co-indexing entry note]: "Matching Media to Audience Equals Marketing Success." Conley, Kathleen, and Toni Tucker. Co-published simultaneously in *College & Undergraduate Libraries* (The Haworth Information Press, an imprint of The Haworth Press, Inc.) Vol. 12, No. 1/2, 2005, pp. 47-64; and: *Real-Life Marketing and Promotion Strategies in College Libraries: Connecting with Campus and Community* (ed: Barbara Whitney Petruzzelli) The Haworth Information Press, an imprint of The Haworth Press, Inc., 2005, pp. 47-64. Single or multiple copies of this article are available for a fee from The Haworth Document Delivery Service [1-800-HAWORTH, 9:00 a.m. - 5:00 p.m. (EST). E-mail address: docdelivery@haworthpress.com].

Available online at http://www.haworthpress.com/web/CUL
© 2005 by The Haworth Press, Inc. All rights reserved.
doi:10.1300/J106v12n01_04

KEYWORDS. Audiences, target market, target audience, market, marketing, marketing plan, academic libraries, promotion, public relations, communication

INTRODUCTION

Faculty and student researchers should understand the inherent value that academic library collections, services, and professional expertise contribute toward scholarly productivity and educational enrichment. Yet, declining gate counts and fewer queries at the reference desk indicate that users are going elsewhere for information. Libraries face competition from ubiquitous Internet access, online availability of full-text scholarship from subscription databases, and even the comfortable sociability offered by coffeehouse bookstores. Many people now depend on a parallel universe of information, easily accessible and satisfying, independent of libraries. A corporate CEO states that his employees have "developed a culture of self-sufficiency, learning to locate the information that they need on their own. People are empowered by computers so that they can find what they need quickly and easily" (Shamel 2002, 61). Stereotypes of librarians, perpetuated even recently by media advertising depicting the "bun-wearing, glasses on a chain, sensibly shod" librarian, pose additional barriers to the recognition and understanding of the true value of librarians (Shamel 2002, 64).

For academic libraries to thrive amidst competition, they must communicate the benefits of library use to users and potential users. Students and faculty should recognize that libraries are useful and welcoming places where they can check out books and DVDs or even laptop computers, receive assistance with challenging research investigations, get answers to factual or directional questions, and friendly, clear instructions on how to navigate a wide variety of information resources. Ideally, users will come to acknowledge the importance of "verified, summarized, and formatted information delivered in a timely cost effective way" provided by librarians (Shamel 2002, 67). A challenge then, is to market not only specific resources and services, but also the overall value of the library and librarians, to diverse audiences. To market successfully, a clear definition and understanding of target audiences must be paired with appropriately selected media and specifically tailored messages.

Marketing tends to be a responsibility undertaken informally, if at all, in academic libraries. Marshall (2001, 118) found, in a survey of academic library directors, that those responsible for public relations in their libraries had limited training and background. Only six of 13 had received any formal education in this area; five of the six had attended workshops or conference presentations targeted primarily to public librarians. Nor do librarians receive adequate marketing training in library schools (Shamel 2002, 64). Tenopir (2002, 13) notes that while information skills are easily and frequently taught in these schools, "positive attitudes about selling yourself, recognizing the needs of the organization, and building customer loyalty are not as common in LIS schools–nor as easily taught."

Constraints on spending in higher education argue against allocating funds to marketing activities. Public investment in higher education has been declining even as demands for services, resources, and access has been escalating (Wedgeworth 2000, 531). Additionally, marketing may not be considered a serious or needed academic pursuit. Some librarians believe that academic library users are a "captive audience" who need to use the library to be successful. Still others believe that promotional activities will increase demands on resources and services that current staffing and budgeting levels cannot support (Dugan 2000, 11).

DEFINITION OF MARKETING

The term "marketing" is often used interchangeably with "public relations." There are many definitions for each concept. According to the web-based tutorial *Marketing the Library* (Noack), "marketing is customer-oriented and has a primary purpose of selling a product. PR concentrates more on selling the library as a whole, developing a corporate identity or image and disseminating a clear message to the community about library mission and goals." For the purposes of marketing in academic libraries, the following definition is relevant:

> Marketing is the wide range of activities involved in making sure that you're continuing to meet the needs of your customers and getting value in return. These activities include market research to find out, for example, what groups of potential customers exist, what their needs, are, which of those needs you can meet, how you should meet them, etc. Marketing also includes analyzing the competition, positioning your new product or service (finding your market niche), pricing your products and services, and promoting

them through continued advertising, promotions, public relations and sales. (McNamara 1999)

McCarthy (1981) described a marketing mix composed of "Four Ps": product, price, place, and promotion, which applies to marketing in academic libraries. "Product" is the value that librarians add through their knowledge, expertise, and informational, organizational, and retrieval skills. The "price" of library services or products consists of both the staff time spent in ensuring that resources and services are available and accessible and the user's time in finding and using resources efficiently. "Place" can be virtual or bricks and mortar. "Promotion" involves advertising, public relations, and matching medium to audience. Successful pairing of media and audiences requires market research and assessment which will be discussed briefly below.

A third concept in the marketing definition involves analyzing the competition, which is necessary in order to define what libraries do more competently, quickly, and satisfactorily than other information providers.

RATIONALE FOR MARKETING

Libraries are not the only nor the first information source sought out by knowledge seekers. Hughes (2000) notes that librarians occupy "competitive space" in the world of information service suppliers. College students explore the Internet, relax at mega bookstores with a latte and a laptop, or consult with their friends for homework help. Course management software that ties syllabi directly to readings and databases may reinforce the notion that it is not necessary to visit the library to complete assignments. Online commercial collections of course-supported materials which offer online tutoring or a smorgasbord of resources for research assistance reinforce the concept of one-stop-shopping for students. Shamel (2002, 65) writes that "competitors are those who anticipate customer demands and satisfy them before the librarians do. Anyone the customer perceives can meet these needs, whether the customer is correct or not, is a competitor."

Marketing can help change negative perceptions of the library and also reinforce positive ones. Marketing research can make librarians aware of how their users perceive current services, resources, or staff. An important goal of library marketing activities is to lead users to the discovery that libraries and librarians can satisfy a wide range of information needs and can give expert personal instruction and assistance.

DEVELOPING A MARKETING PLAN

Successful marketing allows the organization to allocate resources and design programs according to user needs and requires a plan guided by the library's mission and goals. The marketing plan should be an integral part of the library's strategic plan (Dodsworth 1998, 320). The library's mission statement, which should complement the university's mission of teaching, research, and service, can be used as an overall guide for developing a marketing plan. Marketing activities should be undertaken not just because they might be "good for the library," but because they can meaningfully contribute to fulfilling library and institutional missions.

Although there is no one definitive marketing plan format, several elements commonly appear. For example, Kassel (1999) suggests the following:

- prepare a mission statement;
- list and describe target or niche markets;
- describe your services;
- spell out marketing and promotional strategies;
- identify and understand the competition;
- establish marketing goals that are quantifiable; and
- monitor your results carefully.

Before a marketing plan is developed, it is necessary to define targeted markets or audiences and identify their needs. It is important to determine what users themselves want, not what librarians want for them or what librarians think users want. The needs of various target markets can be identified through the use of market research techniques. Librarians can administer surveys; conduct phone or face-to-face interviews; keep transaction logs; analyze database usage or circulation records; study patterns in e-mail, chat, or in-person reference; hold focus groups; consult local census and campus demographic information; offer suggestion boxes; and share anecdotal evidence. Market research as part of a well-thought-out marketing plan will most likely combine several of the aforementioned activities.

Additionally, librarians should ask the following questions to ascertain their ability to carry out an aggressive marketing plan:

- Is there physical space available for events with adequate seating, lighting, and technology?
- Is there space for displays or exhibits?
- How will marketing literature be made available to library visitors and to target audiences on- and off-campus?
- What are the important media outlets and who are the best contacts at each?
- Is there adequate budget support for promotional activities?
- Is there support among the library staff for marketing?
- Who will be responsible for carrying out the library's marketing plan?

Answer to these and other questions will reveal the library's potential for marketing success.

IDENTIFYING TARGETED MARKETS

It is important to differentiate among audiences because they bring different expectations, and have different actual and perceived needs for library service. There are myriad ways to label targeted markets. Markets can be divided simply into primary/secondary or internal/external. The obvious primary audience for an academic library comprises students, faculty, and staff. Secondary markets are those outside the university community who have an interest in the library or use its resources or services. Internal markets are those with a direct connection to the university, such as administrators, students, faculty and staff, Friends, or alumni groups. External markets include those individuals or agencies not directly associated with the university such as community leaders, media outlets, or other schools or colleges.

In synthesizing the work of others, Besant and Sharp (2000, 17, 20-21) suggest a different approach, that of identifying markets by relationship. They define relationship marketing as a mutual interest between company and customer. Relationship marketing emphasizes customer retention and the establishment of long-term customer relationships. Library workers form and maintain relationships from the following:

- Customer Markets
- Internal Markets (employees and departments in the library)
- Supplier and Alliance Markets (publishers, vendors, and book sellers)
- Referral Markets (word-of-mouth by satisfied customers)
- Recruitment Markets (attracting and training quality employees)
- Influence Markets (boards of directors, trustees, friends groups and legislators)

De Sáez (2002, 115-35) proposes yet another way of segmenting markets, by specifying geographic, demographic, behavioral, psychographic, and lifestyle groups. She suggests that a market segment needs to satisfy certain criteria in order to be targeted successfully; the segment should be homogenous, accessible, and measurable.

Whichever typology is employed, market segmentation can lead to better use of resources and services because different promotional strategies, employing different messages and media, are directed to meet the needs of specific groups of library users.

TARGETED MARKETS AT ILLINOIS STATE UNIVERSITY

Illinois State University (ISU) is located in the twin cities of Bloomington/Normal, with a population of nearly 150,000. One of twelve public universities in Illinois, ISU is a student-centered, multi-purpose institution committed to providing undergraduate and graduate programs of the highest quality. The University enrolls over 20,000 students from 49 states and 71 countries. ISU's academic programs are supported by the services and collections of Milner Library containing over 3,000,000 volumes; the library employs 33 librarians and 84 staff.

At ISU, a designated librarian has primary responsibilities for grant-writing and public relations. A Public Relations (PR) Committee supports this position. The PR Committee's charge is to communicate the library's value by identifying audiences and aggressively marketing to them. Membership on the committee includes library faculty and administrative and civil service representatives (paraprofessionals). Milner Library's liaison from the campus development office and the assistant director of alumni services have been consulted for specific activities such as homecoming and receptions at state professional conferences.

Initially, the committee identified two categories of audiences: internal and external. These audiences were determined to be those that were served as part of the library and university missions or those audiences that used the library frequently or had a relationship with the library. Internal audiences included students, faculty, library and university support staff and administrators. External groups identified include ISU alumni, Friends of Milner Library, community institutions of higher education, library consortia, media, elected officials, library vendors, and because ISU is a public institution, citizens of Illinois. As the PR committee is tasked with promoting new library services or activities, audiences may be added or refined.

The identification of external audiences required extensive brainstorming by the PR committee. Most members of the PR committee have many years of library, teaching, or administrative experience. This experience was crucial in identifying audiences. The committee scrutinized potential audience groups and combined or eliminated some. Those eliminated were groups that only occasionally use the library, such as high school students or the local genealogy society.

The committee next determined which media communicated most effectively with each audience. (See Appendix A.) The PR Committee brainstormed about each audience and how each group accessed information. Members of each audience were asked informally how they obtained information about campus activities. The students interviewed cited that they read the campus newspaper, the *Daily Vidette*, and electronic signs around campus. Recently, students suggested to the library that we "chalk" campus sidewalks to announce programs.

Other media tools were selected by observing how faculty, staff, and the public gather information. Like selecting audiences, this process is fluid and changes with different activities. Faculty read the *ISU Report* for campus news and the public notices posted in local businesses; library faculty and staff are reached effectively through e-mail or internal electronic publications. If attendance at an event is low or a library service is under-used, the PR committee either targets additional identified audiences or selects different tools for communicating.

The following sections provide a brief description of Milner Library audience segments, examples of media used to communicate a service, program, or activity, and a tip to facilitate working with that particular audience.

INTERNAL AUDIENCES

Students

A student is any person registered for classes at Illinois State University. Many types of media are used for students because students communicate and access information in a variety of ways. Because contacts differ for each media type and change from time to time, it is important to continually update the list of contacts. The Public Relations Committee at Milner Library added a new communication tool when a reduction in library hours had to be disseminated to the campus. The committee looked at the best way to communicate the change to students. While negotiating to have the message posted on electronic signs in campus food courts, a resident hall staff member suggested that the best way to reach students would be to use a service called Campus Connections, a closed circuit TV system located in each residence hall room. Survey results showed that this system reaches 90% of residence hall students.

Tip: Inquire about tools that other departments use to get the word out to students. Don't miss a valuable resource by relying solely on the usual newsletters or flyers.

Faculty

Faculty refers to any individual in a ranked or unranked appointment for the purpose of instruction, organized research, or public service in an academic (credit-hour producing) department or academic support area. Communicating with faculty can be as difficult as or even more difficult than communicating with students because of faculty's diverse teaching schedules and ways of accessing information. When faculty needed to be informed quickly about the change in library hours, the university president's office suggested that the best way to reach the most faculty was a broadcast e-mail. On the ISU campus, broadcast e-mail is used very sparingly. However, the library's message was considered important enough to use this communication tool.

Tip: If you believe your message is vitally important, others will, also.

Library Personnel

One of the most important audiences is library faculty and staff. Nothing can inhibit the promotion of new products, services, or events more than uninformed library personnel. An employee newsletter can be an excellent way to get the word out to this audience. Speakers, new services, or changes in services can all be discussed in this type of publication. Milner Library's internal newsletter, *Admin News*, is e-mailed to each library faculty and staff member on a bi-monthly basis. Because of the frequency of this newsletter, word gets out in a timely manner.

Tip: A library's best promotional tool is word-of-mouth from its own personnel. Be sure staff receive updates on library activities on a timely basis and in an easily accessible format.

Illinois State University Staff

Our PR Committee defined all other non-library university employees, from hourly to administrative positions, as staff. At ISU, we found that the highest numbers of non-library, non-faculty personnel fall into the state university's civil service category. Using the civil service newsletter is an effective way to reach this wide range of people to inform them about what's happening at the library. Beyond encouraging attendance at library events, providing library information in the civil service newsletter is beneficial to staff because many are enrolled in university classes and need to become efficient library users.

University administrators are another important audience in this group. During National Library Week, the Public Relations Committee ordered cookies decorated with the international library symbol from a local retail establishment and had them delivered to university administrative offices with a note thanking them for their continued support of the library.

Tip: Providing food with the library's message is a good strategy.

EXTERNAL AUDIENCES

Alumni

Graduates of Illinois State University comprise our alumni market. Alumni are allowed to use the library and receive a library courtesy card. It is hoped that they will provide financial support to the university, making them an important group to keep apprised of and involved in library activities. Several tools are available to reach this far-ranging group, including the *Alumni Magazine*. The chair of the library's Public Relations Committee sits on the editorial board of this publication. Consequently, the magazine has run several feature stories along with many short news pieces about the library. One article traced the history of the library, highlighting our first librarian and namesake Ange Milner. Another issue ran a feature on the university's archivist, a library faculty member. The magazine can also be used to publicize new collections or grants the library has received. This coverage increases alumni awareness of the library which may help them keep the library in mind during fundraising efforts. Library personnel attend alumni receptions when possible, an excellent opportunity for face-to-face communication. Alumni can have fond memories of the library and may want their financial contributions directed to help support the library.

Tip: Former students can be loyal supporters; keep in touch with them.

Parents

This much neglected audience is defined as those who provide support to students attending the university. Why do we consider them an audience? Because they are intrinsically interested in their students' academic success, making parents aware of library services can only help the library serve students better. "Milner Library Parent's Guide" is a brochure that describes library services and answers frequently asked questions, including cost of printing, library hours, and research assistance. The library distributes this brochure during a required two-day orientation session for parents and their entering freshmen. The library also uses this opportunity to answer questions about the library.

Tip: Parents need to know that the library will provide student support and cares about their students' academic success.

Community Institutions of Higher Learning

This group is defined as any institution of higher education in the surrounding Bloomington/Normal community. Institutions include two four-year liberal arts universities and one community college. Libraries have shared materials for years, but shared programming is unusual. To increase awareness of the university libraries in the Bloomington/Normal community, Illinois State University and Illinois Wesleyan University (ISU) work together to bring nationally known authors to speak on both campuses. The deans of ISU and IWU libraries met to discuss ways the two university libraries could cooperate on programming. Bringing in authors seemed like a natural and logical activity in which the libraries could partner. Thus, one institution did not have to bear the entire cost or make all of the arrangements. The first two shared authors were a resounding success. The events gave greater visibility to both of these university libraries and community members frequently inquire about who the next author will be. This now annual fall event has brought in Joyce Carol Oates, Molly Ivins, and Garrison Keillor.

Tip: Don't think of other libraries as competitors, think of them as partners. Partnering can enhance programming or other opportunities that cannot easily be accomplished by a single library because of staffing or financial constraints.

Library Consortia

Consortia can consist of one type of library or a combination of academic, public, school, or special libraries. This is a peer-to-peer audience, comprising librarians and support staff working in a variety of libraries with many different skills and strengths. Consortia can be local, regional, or state-based and may exist to support the sharing of an online union catalog, continuing education activities, or collection development. Milner librarians actively participate in their regional consortium, the Alliance Library System, and the system posts Milner's programs such as author visits and workshops, on its electronic newsletter, *e-Glance*, and distributes flyers that go to over three hundred libraries.

Tip: Consortia members are an audience that can benefit from networking and attention. They can help share information through list servs, by posting flyers in their institutions, and word-of-mouth.

Media Outlets

The media includes print, audio, and video. To be effective in marketing and promotion initiatives, libraries must develop strong relationships with both on-campus and community-based media. Most universities have a department devoted to public relations, staffed with professionals who are experts in media relations. Librarians should get to know the staff in this department and learn how to best work with them. Campus media relations staff is one of the library's most important audiences because they can be enlisted to extend the reach of the library's own publicity. If they are kept informed about library happenings, new services, speakers, unusual collections, grants or awards received, they can help promote these activities. But don't expect them to do all the work. Ask for assistance in writing news releases and how to best market a service or program, and find out what the limits of their services are.

The next step is building relationships with the local non-campus-based media. Most newspapers will have a beat reporter for higher education. Find out who that person is and meet with them. Ask what types of stories they are looking for. Let them know that the library uses the campus public relations department, but also let them know who to call if they have questions about a story involving the library. Last year, our local paper ran two front page articles and three "Focus" (a feature section of the paper) pieces about Milner Library. Stories do not have to be about a major event or activity. However, the public is generally not interested in activities that impact only the campus. What is the library doing that would interest or benefit the community? Human interest stories can be one way to get the library's name out.

Tip: Think about how to describe library events and services in a way that focuses on the benefits to the general public.

Elected Officials

These are the men and women elected to represent the community at the local, state, and national level. A percent of public university funding comes from state and national government resources. Many profit and non-profit groups lobby lawmakers at both the state and national levels. Pretending that academic libraries are above this practice will only ensure that they are overlooked when tax dollars are doled out. Academic libraries must put themselves forward to get the word out about the importance of what they do and their funding needs for buildings, collections, programming, or equipment. In doing so, public officials will be educated about the benefits to their constituents of funding for academic libraries.

The lobbying process does not have to take a lot of time. The American Library Association already coordinates Legislative Days; most state library organizations arrange State Legislative Days. Become involved with these events and learn from them. Invite legislators to all library events; even if they never show up, they will at least know the library is active and the library's name will become familiar. After a while, they might attend to see what really is going on. Milner Library has pursued this strategy, and at least one elected official, from city council members to mayors to state and federal representatives, attends every event. At a reception recognizing international students, all state and local representatives were invited as usual. The mayor, two city council members, and two state representatives attended. Since that event, there has been an increase in representatives' attendance at library activities.

Another way to get the library's needs known is through Federal Initiatives (proposals to a state's Congressional Delegation requesting funding to support projects within the institution). Most large universities submit Federal Initiatives to federal representatives and government agencies. Find out who on your campus initiates this process and meet with them. It is the library's responsibility to seek out elected officials and get the word out about academic libraries and their needs.

Tip: Personal contacts are an effective means of communication with elected officials. Letters help, but building personal relationships is the best practice.

Vendors

In the most basic definition, vendor means a seller. Library vendors deserve recognition because they are partners in providing resources such as databases, periodical subscriptions, and monographs to library patrons. It is mutually beneficial for the library and vendors to work together to provide the best product. Milner Library faced a crisis when many of its periodical subscriptions lapsed due to the bankruptcy of its subscription vendor. When hundreds of publishers continued to send periodicals, pending resolution of the financial problem, Milner sent a letter to each individual publisher thanking them for their support. It's good relationship-building to say thank you when vendors do something good for the benefit of the patrons.

Tip: Libraries must stop thinking of vendors as adversaries but rather as partners in providing information to our patrons.

Community

People who live near the campus are considered community users. At Illinois State University, anyone living within a fifty mile radius is eligible for a library courtesy card. The card allows citizens to check out library materials. Community members are invited, through articles in the local paper, public service announcements on local radio stations, and flyers posted at coffee shops and businesses, to all library programming. And they attend regularly. When children's author/illustrator Tomie dePaola spoke in the library, 450 people attended; Molly Ivins drew a crowd of 375.

Tip: Community members can be strong supporters of academic library events, and may even become members of the Friends or commit to other financial support.

AUDIENCE SUMMARY

Each audience plays a key role in the academic library community. It is important that libraries know their audiences and what type of media is most effective in reaching each of them. Knowing your audience is more complex than making a list of who the library serves and matching them to media. It involves exploring who the library is really serving or who the library should be serving, knowing what services need to be marketed to different audiences, and knowing which media has the biggest impact on each audience. It includes looking for and utilizing new media, scouting out innovative ways to get the library's message out.

The Public Relations Committee at Milner Library follows a standard process when announcing a new service, a change in services, or an event. After developing the message, the committee, uses a "Brainstorming Worksheet" to identify the audiences that need to be reached, what media will be used for each audience, and what the proper message should be. (See Appendix B.)

When faced with a reduction in library hours, the committee listed key audiences as students, faculty, and staff. Next, the committee looked at the matrix of media choices previously determined to best fit each audience. After reviewing the matrix, the committee realized that an additional media tool was needed to reach as many off-campus students as possible. We reasoned that the bookstores near campus might be a good outlet since every student purchases textbooks. Both bookstores agreed to include a half-sheet flyer explaining the new library hours with each purchase during the first week of classes. This method of communication would not work for all messages, but it proved effective in this instance. Each message needs to be looked at individually; media are selected based on the specific message and the particular audience that needs to hear it. Word about the hours reduction caused a buzz on campus. Students did get the message. If they didn't hear about the reduction in library hours from designated media, they heard about it through other students and faculty. Successful marketing will take on a life of its own, generating word-of-mouth communication, which carries the library's message beyond the medium.

QUICK BIB

Besant, Larry X., and Deborah Sharp. 2000. Libraries need relationship marketing. *Information Outlook* 4 (3): 17-22.
Noack, Deana. 2003-2004. Marketing the library. Ohio Library Foundation.
http://www.olc.org/marketing/.
Shamel, Cynthia L. 2002. Building a brand: Got librarian? *Searcher* 10 (7):
60-76. http://www.infotoday.com/searcher/jul02/shamel.htm.

REFERENCES

Besant, Larry X., and Deborah Sharp. 2000. Libraries need relationship marketing. *Information Outlook* 4 (3):17-22.
De Sáez, Eileen Elliott. 2002. Market segmentation. In *Marketing concepts for libraries and information services*, London: Facet Pub. 2nd ed., 115-35.
Dodsworth, Ellen. 1998. Marketing Academic Libraries: A necessary plan. *The Journal of Academic Librarianship* 24 (4): 320-2.
Dugan, Charlotte. 1994. Virtually possible: Academic library public relations. *Techni-
calities* 14 (6): 10-12.
Hughes, Carol Ann. 2000. Information services for higher education. *D-Lib Magazine*
6 (12), http://www.dlib.org/dlib/december00/hughes/12hughes.html.
Kassel, Amelia. 1999. How to write a marketing plan. *Marketing Library Services* 13 (5),
http://infotoday.com/mls/jun99/how-to.htm.
McCarthy, E. Jerome. 1981. *Basic marketing: A managerial approach.* Homewood,
Ill: Richard D. Irwin.
McNamara, Carter. 1999. Basic definitions: Advertising, marketing, promotion, public
and publicity, and sales. http://www.mapnp.org/library/ad_prmot/defntion.htm.
Marshall, Nancy J. 2001. Public relations in academic libraries: A descriptive analysis.
The Journal of Academic Librarianship 27 (2): 116-21.
Noack, Deana. 2003-2004. Marketing the library. Ohio Library Foundation. http://
www.olc.org/marketing/.
Shamel, Cynthia L. 2002. Building a brand: Got librarian? *Searcher* 10 (7): 60-76.
http://www.infotoday.com/searcher/jul02/shamel.htm.
Tenopir, Carol. 2002. Educating tomorrow's informational professionals today. *Searcher*
10 (7): 12-20. http://www.infotoday.com/searcher/jul02/tenopir.htm.
Wedgeworth, Robert. 2000. Donor relations as public relations: Toward a philosophy
of fund-raising. *Library Trends* 48 (3): 530-39.

APPENDIX A. Communications Grid–Matching Media to Audiences

Milner Library Public Relations Committee
Illinois State University

Media → / Audience ↓	Vidette	Campus Connections	Flyers	Brochures	Newsletters	Bulletin Boards	Electronic Signs	Posters	TV 10	Radio	Lib Web Site	ISU Web Site	ISU Report	Word-of-Mouth	Pantagraph	E-mail
Internal																
Students	X	X	X	X	X	X	X	X	X	X	X	X		X	X	
Faculty	X		X	X	X	X	X	X	X	X	X	X	X	X	X	X
Library Personnel	X		X		X	X	X	X	X	X	X	X	X	X	X	X
ISU Staff & Admin.	X		X		X	X	X	X	X	X	X	X	X	X	X	X
External																
Alumni					X						X	X	X		X	X
Friends of Milner				X	X						X	X	X		X	X
Parents				X	X						X	X			X	X
Community Inst.			X		X		X	X	X		X	X	X		X	X	X
Library Consortia			X		X			X			X	X	X		X	X
Citizens of Illinois											X	X	X	·		
Media											X	X	X		X	X	X
Elected Officials											X	X		X	X	X
Vendors																X

Media Definitions:
Vidette–Illinois State University daily campus newspaper
Campus Connections–Closed circuit television in residence halls
TV 10–Student-run television newscast with live daily programming
Pantagraph–Local daily newspaper for the Bloomington/Normal community

APPENDIX B. Brainstorming Worksheet for Library Hours Reduction

Milner Library Public Relations Committee
Illinois State University

Date: <u>August 2003</u>
Message: <u>Reduction in Library Hours</u>

Audience(s):

1. Students
2. Faculty
3. ISU Staff
4. Community
5.
6.

Media:

1. The Daily Vidette
2. Campus Connections
3. ISU Report
4. Milner Library Electronic Sign
5. Prairie Room Electronic Sign (Student Center)
6. Milner Library Web Site
7. ISU Web Site
8. Information Sheets with talking points at public service desks
9. 3,000 1/2 sheet flyers distributed from Barnes & Noble College Book Store and the Alamo Book Store in downtown Normal
10.
11.

Marketing Virtual Reference:
What Academic Libraries Have Done

Luke Vilelle

SUMMARY. The honeymoon between virtual reference and academic libraries is over. Now comes the hard part–making sure, through effective marketing, that our users are aware of the benefits that the service can provide to them. Marketing has received increased attention in the library literature in recent years, and many authors describe what their libraries have done to promote virtual reference. However, these descriptions are often buried within larger works. This article draws from the literature a variety of real-life examples of marketing the service, in an effort to foster ideas and conversation about how best to increase awareness of virtual reference. *[Article copies available for a fee from The Haworth Document Delivery Service: 1-800-HAWORTH. E-mail address: <docdelivery@haworthpress.com> Website: <http://www.HaworthPress.com> © 2005 by The Haworth Press, Inc. All rights reserved.]*

KEYWORDS. Virtual reference, marketing, promotions, publicity, academic libraries

Luke Vilelle (MLIS, University of Pittsburgh) is Outreach Librarian, Virginia Tech University Libraries, Blacksburg, VA 24062 (address e-mail to: lvilelle@vt.edu).
The author offers a special thanks to Elizabeth Mahoney of the University of Pittsburgh for helping to guide the research process.

[Haworth co-indexing entry note]: "Marketing Virtual Reference: What Academic Libraries Have Done." Vilelle, Luke. Co-published simultaneously in *College & Undergraduate Libraries* (The Haworth Information Press, an imprint of The Haworth Press, Inc.) Vol. 12, No. 1/2, 2005, pp. 65-79; and: *Real-Life Marketing and Promotion Strategies in College Libraries: Connecting with Campus and Community* (ed: Barbara Whitney Petruzzelli) The Haworth Information Press, an imprint of The Haworth Press, Inc., 2005, pp. 65-79. Single or multiple copies of this article are available for a fee from The Haworth Document Delivery Service [1-800-HAWORTH, 9:00 a.m. - 5:00 p.m. (EST). E-mail address: docdelivery@haworthpress.com].

Available online at http://www.haworthpress.com/web/CUL
© 2005 by The Haworth Press, Inc. All rights reserved.
doi:10.1300/J106v12n01_05

INTRODUCTION

In the past few years, the tone of articles on virtual reference services in academic libraries has shifted from giddily optimistic to cautiously optimistic to neutral. Much of this change has been due to the relatively small number of users. Janes found, in his census of 162 chat reference services, that the median number of virtual reference questions (including e-mail and chat) was six per day per service (2003). Those numbers seemed low to many in the library profession, and the lack of usage has led to hand-wringing.

But instead of simply asking whether or not to discontinue chat reference services, perhaps we also need to explore whether library users have been adequately informed about the benefits of using chat reference. In other words, have we marketed the services effectively? Maxwell argues that users never wanted chat reference in the first place (2004, 40-41). Coffman and Arret acknowledge that "marketing works" and that probably every library could do a better job of marketing, but then argue that the demise of well-marketed web-based reference companies–such as WebHelp–means that the upside to be gained from marketing chat reference is limited (2004). Unlike extinct commercial Web reference sites, however, libraries already have a well-established reputation of helping people find information. Perhaps libraries, many of which have little marketing experience, simply need a better marketing strategy. Unfortunately, the literature on marketing virtual reference is limited, and much is restricted to two or three paragraphs buried within larger articles about starting or evaluating chat reference.

To provide academic libraries with concrete ideas for marketing their chat reference services, I conducted a literature review. I limited the review to publications appearing between 2002 through 2004, and to academic libraries–though some resources on virtual reference collaboratives refer to both public and academic libraries. I focused primarily on case studies, though I have also cited advice from other extensive marketing sources. Both traditional library and information science indexing sources as well as web sites such as The Teaching Librarian (http://www.teachinglibrarian.org), The Virtual Reference Desk (http://www.vrd.org), and Bernie Sloan's Digital Reference Services Bibliography (http://www.lis.uiuc.edu/~b-sloan/digiref.html) proved useful in uncovering relevant publications.

In sharing the results of this review, I have grouped activities into eight marketing categories: target markets, branding/naming, ongoing marketing, collaboration, promotional materials, promotional events, publicity, and word-of-mouth. (Although many of the items in the last four categories are complementary, I separated them to make distinctions among the types of promotional efforts used for virtual reference.) Two quick reference charts (see Tables 1 and 2) show the promotional items and publicity used at various institutions to promote virtual reference. In addition, a list of the web sites for all of the virtual reference services mentioned in this article is provided in the Appendix so readers may review those services more fully. For the purposes of this literature review, promotional materials are defined as objects that can be taken home by library users; promotional events are defined as outreach efforts that have a specific time frame or setting; and publicity is mass communication to users. Keep in mind that other marketing techniques may have been used to promote virtual reference in academic libraries, but this article covers only those promotional efforts that have been described in the literature.

TABLE 1. Promotional Materials Used for Virtual Reference

	Table Tents	Post-It Notes	Bookmarks	Flyers	Postcards/ Mailings	Brochures
ASERL			X	X	X	
CPP	X		X	X		
CSF				X		
Case				X	X	X
Illinois			X	X		X
Kansas			X	X	X	
LSU			X	X		
NJ			X	X		
SC				X		
SU	X			X		
UA	X	X	X	X		
UI				X		
Wash*			X		X	

*The state of Washington also provided magnets, pencils and pens, bags, buttons, and static cling stickers.
NOTE: See Appendix for full names of institutions listed above.

TABLE 2. Publicity Used for Virtual Reference

	Information Literacy Classes	Press Release/ News Stories	Newspaper Ads	Radio Ads/ PSAs	Electric Message Boards	Endorsements	Sandwich Boards	Chalk Sidewalks*
ASERL		X						
CPP	X	X			X			
Case	X	X						
Illinois		X	X	X				
Kansas		X				X		
LSU		X	X	X				
NJ		X						
SC			X	X				
SU		X	X					X
UA	X							
UI		X						
Wash			X	X			X	

*Using chalk to write messages on campus sidewalks.
NOTE: See Appendix for full names of institutions listed above.

TARGET MARKETS

Coffman stresses the importance of targeting markets: "the first step in developing any marketing program–whether for virtual reference services or orange juice–is to sit down and segment your users, to (1) figure out what groups of users you want to serve and what their various needs and wants are, (2) determine how your services can help meet those needs, and (3) identify marketing approaches that may be best suited to reaching each of your many audiences" (2003, 77). He also notes that all libraries will have at least two segments in common: patrons who already use library services, and those who do not.

The University of Arizona Library identified three primary markets for its virtual reference service: users of their new information commons, undergraduate students, and students enrolled in distance education (Bracke 2003). For each market, they created promotional materials designed with those students in mind. For users of the information commons, Arizona created table tents, a desktop icon, and Post-It Notes. To reach undergraduate students, Arizona utilized student employee training to increase word-of-mouth promotion of the service, class instruction, and space in the library's welcome tent at orientation. For distance learners, Arizona placed bookmarks in the books sent to them and created flyers for satellite campus classrooms.

The marketing guidelines developed for the University of Washington and the King County (WA) Library System by Girvin Strategic Branding & Design also emphasize the importance of targeted marketing. For a target market, both demographics and psychographics should be identified: for example, if a college were to target undergrads, the demographics might state the market is "between the ages of 18-20, ethnically diverse, and includes distance learners from surrounding states." The psychographics, or lifestyle characteristics, might include "very comfortable using computers, technology and the Internet; have heard about or participated in live chat; under deadline" (2003, 13-14).

BRANDING/NAMING

The Girvin marketing guidelines identify the two types of branding that can be used when creating a virtual reference service. The most common among academic libraries has been the creation of a "sub-brand," where the service is marketed under the "parent brand" of the library. At the other end of the spectrum, the service can be marketed as a "stand-alone brand," with few or no obvious connections to the parent library. The guidelines identify advantages and disadvantages to each strategy, but perhaps the most crucial difference is this: if a library hopes to reach patrons who are already familiar with the parent brand, then a sub-branding strategy is most likely the best option. If a library hopes to reach new users through virtual reference, then a stand-alone brand should be considered (2002, 7-10).

Closely tied to the concept of branding is the selection of a program name. The name plays a large role in how the service is perceived by users. The Girvin guidelines break names into two categories–descriptive or evocative. Descriptive names, such as "Ask A Librarian" and "Homework Help," are straightforward and describe the service. Evocative names, such as "Yahoo!," can evoke a tone or personality, but do not necessarily have direct associations attached with them (2002, 21-22).

Although I found no references to purely evocative names for virtual reference services, "KANAnswer"–used by a consortium of Kansas academic and public libraries–is an example of a name that includes both evocative and descriptive aspects. The web address, http://www. kananswer.com, takes a patron to the virtual reference site, where a user will find graphics created specifically to showcase their service (Stockham, Turtle, and Hansen 2002/2003, 260).

At individual academic libraries, it is more common to connect virtual reference with other reference services. In this approach, digital reference is tied graphically and intellectually to a library's in-person and telephone reference offerings. By doing so, the library hopes to capitalize on the reference reputation it has previously built.

Names such as "Ask A Librarian," "AskRef," "AskNow," "AskLive," and "Ask a Question" predominate. A scan of academic library web sites in December 2002 revealed that of the 128 services viewed, thirty-three (39 percent) had chosen "Ask A Librarian" (Duncan and Fichter 2004, 223). However, Kawakami argues that "more memorable names might be catchier," identifying as examples "RefeXpress," "Q&A Café," "Q&A NJ," "Instant Librarian," and "Ready for Reference" (2002, 29). A recent study conducted by the Health Sciences Library at the University of Saskatchewan reached a different conclusion. A survey of users prior to starting a chat reference service found that "Ask A Librarian," "Click Here," and "Ask Me NOW" had the most appeal. Phrases including the word "answers" misled many survey participants, who tended to think a link including that word would lead to a frequently asked question list (Duncan and Fichter 2004, 220).

ONGOING MARKETING

A theme repeated throughout the literature is the importance of continually marketing the service in academic libraries because of the "transitory nature of the student population" (Kratzert, Richey, and Wasserman 2001, 80). Word-of-mouth marketing becomes critical in this effort, because most libraries cannot afford to continually pump dollars into advertising their services. Barber and Wallace included this advice among their ten tips for marketing virtual reference services (VRS): "prepare and encourage all frontline staff to put in a plug for VRS at every opportunity . . . Ask 10 satisfied customers to tell 10 friends. Also encourage Friends and trustees to spread the word." They also address the importance of ongoing marketing by suggesting that libraries "collect testimonials to use in your next wave of publicity" (2002, 1).

KANAnswer included ongoing marketing plans as part of its startup proposal. This continuous publicity would include "demonstrations at conferences, updated web pages (including 'what's new' banners), periodic mailings, and testimonials" (Stockham, Turtle, and Hansen 2002/ 2003, 261).

Kawakami also stressed the importance of continued marketing. She suggests educating the staff to regularly promote the service in all interactions with patrons–at the circulation desk, at the reference desk, in bibliographic instruction (2002, 29).

Other ideas for ongoing promotion include issuing announcements to new and continuing students through campus e-mail and posting permanent flyers near computers designated for patron use (Kratzert, Richey, and Wasserman 2001, 80). The Association of Southeast Research Libraries' (ASERL) v-Ref service proposal recommends the investigation of "options for tie-ins with National Library Week and campus events" (2003, 11).

WEB SITE PLACEMENT

Perhaps the most important aspect of ongoing marketing is the design and placement of the virtual reference icon on the library web site. ASERL is just one of many organizations to recommend placing a clickable logo/icon on as many pages as possible–within the library site, in the catalog and journal databases, and even in course management systems such as Blackboard (2003, 11). Try to place the links everywhere a user might need help. Coffman writes that this strategy "has proved to be the single most effective method of marketing virtual reference services, bar none" (2003, 78).

Kawakami shows the demonstrable effect of burying the link to the virtual reference. When UCLA started its pilot program in spring 2001, the link was placed "two clicks down on the pages of the Undergraduate Library and the Biomedical Library." The service received only fourteen callers in the first quarter. After placing the icon on the library home page, calls rose to forty-five in the second quarter and one hundred in the third quarter, suggesting that the improved location of the link was at least a contributing factor to the increased use of the service (2002, 29).

Wells, in her article on Case Western Reserve University's experiences, echoes Kawakami's findings. In the fall of 2001, only thirty-four questions were received. By expanding the number of pages on which the chat button was located, the number of questions increased to ninety-six in the spring of 2002 and to 104 in the fall of 2002 (despite a month of technical difficulties). Wells also studied which chat request buttons generated the most questions–the home page generated 38 percent of the questions, followed by the catalog page with 22 percent and the database pages with 18 percent (2003, 136).

Lindbloom advocates that academic libraries try to place virtual reference icons on distance learning web pages and professors' web pages (2003), and Ronan sees value in approaching student services offices or campus organizations to see if they will link from their home page to the library's chat reference service (2003, 168).

On the page that introduces the digital reference service, how is the service explained? In writing for the web, short and concise copy is paramount, and the most important information must be placed at the top of the page. Making visitors scroll for information should be avoided. The Girvin marketing guidelines demand that web writers keep the service explanation brief: "To ensure that service-related information gets read, we suggest the following process: write, edit and cut, review, edit and cut again!" (2002, 31). Hirko, in her presentation, again stressed the importance of avoiding small, dense text and library jargon. A simple web address and clear, easily understandable text are the objectives (2003).

Related to the goal of web site placement is the creation of a desktop icon or persistent button. Coffman describes how the persistent button works: the user must download a small applet file, which places an icon for the virtual reference service on the patron's desktop computer or directly on the patron's browser bar. This enables the service to be kept in front of patrons even when using web sites not related to the library (2003, 80-81). However, Coffman does not write about usage statistics for such a button, and it seems unlikely that many patrons would be willing to download a file. What libraries can do, however, is place a desktop icon on their public computers. Bracke identified this approach in her presentation. Every public computer in Arizona's Information Commons has a clickable icon on the desktop (2003).

COLLABORATION

One of the best ways to spread the word about virtual reference services is through collaboration with other campus departments. These groups, whether an academic department or student life, "have information needs that you can help with and constituencies they can notify about your service" (Meola and Stormont 2002, 138). Syracuse University's (SU) Web Chat Action Team suggested these specific collaborative opportunities for the SU Library: the Writing Center, the Department of International Programs Abroad, Project Advance (the offering of college courses to qualified high school students), and the Independent Study Degree Program (Coppola et al. 2002, 12). Most colleges and universities will have similar programs, with potential for collaborations, on their campuses.

PROMOTIONAL MATERIALS

Much of the literature surveyed indicated that many libraries employ similar types of promotional items to publicize their virtual reference services.

Some resources offer ideas for maximizing the effectiveness of promotional materials. Ronan's chapter on promotion includes a checklist of possible strategies for both promotional materials and publicity (2003, 165). Ronan, a librarian at the University of Florida, also offers tips for selecting appropriate giveaway items. For instance, choose things "that have a natural link with chat reference, such as a pencil to jot down notes or a mouse pad to sit next to the user's computer." She adds that giveaways should be personalized with a logo, library name, and potentially a URL or e-mail address. In the same vein, she discourages food items such as gum or candy, because any advertising on the wrapper will soon be thrown in the trash (2003, 172).

The Girvin marketing guidelines identify a number of promotional items for chat reference: brochures/leaflets, flyers/posters, direct mail/postcards, newsletters, and giveaways. Its example of a "welcome kit" for college freshmen includes a "guide to online resources, a business card for a 'personal' librarian, testimonials from past freshmen, and a mousepad with the virtual reference service URL" (2002, 66).

Particularly interesting to note from Table 1: fliers posted at Cal State Fullerton proved particularly effective when placed near e-mail terminals (Kratzert, Richey, and Wasserman 2001, 79-80); the New Jersey collaborative distributed bookmarks to local bookstores (Sweet, Lisa, and Colston 2003, 54); the Illinois flyers urged students to "take a librarian home tonight" (Kibbee, Ward, and Ma 2002, 27).

PROMOTIONAL EVENTS

Events can be worrisome because of concerns about attendance. However, Ronan offers ways to make events both fun and promotional. She writes that a special reception or open house can help publicize virtual reference, particularly if held "for important milestones that you reach along the way, such as your 100th or 1000th question." If you would rather not have the hassle of creating a special event, Ronan suggests helping to sponsor a community event to increase awareness of your chat service. Sponsorship can boost name recognition, and give you opportunities to network with users (2003, 168).

Notable among promotional events were those held at Duke University. As a part of a university-wide spring celebration, the library's space featured a "legendary witty and honest librarian with a secret identity who would respond to any query." A computer with wireless access was available for students, and they lined up to ask virtual questions. By the end of the event, the reference librarian had been chatting continuously for almost four hours.

At another outdoor festival, the library "hosted a jeopardy game" using virtual reference software. The librarian in his office asked the questions, while students in their dorms and at a computer set up at the festival competed for prizes. "Again, people seemed to be entertained not only by the competition but by the novelty of using the virtual reference software to play" (Blank 2002/2003, 222-23).

Syracuse University Library created a PowerPoint kiosk presentation for use at outreach sessions, and also conducted demonstrations of the chat reference service in the student center (Coppola et al. 2002, 6-7).

PUBLICITY

Publicity includes both paid advertising, such as direct mail and newspaper and radio advertisements, and free exposure, through venues such as newspaper articles and public service announcements. If deciding to spend money for direct advertisements, the library must consider the most effective medium to reach its audience.

Free publicity can have its own costs–building relationships with reporters in order to sell your story can take time and patience, and you likely will not have final control over the contents. To pitch a story to the press, keep these points in mind: make it interesting and newsworthy; verify the truth of your claims; be sure the reporter's experience is as smooth as possible when testing a service; and document any exposure you do receive, so that it might be used later in communications with target audiences (Girvin 2002, 64).

Direct advertising, as the Girvin marketing guidelines state, generally has higher costs than other public relations efforts. Because of the advertising saturation in today's society, research has shown that it takes nine exposures to an ad to impact the average viewer (Girvin 2002, 67). Paid advertising, then, demands a long-term commitment to be effective.

The Saddleback College librarians recommend promotion through the college radio station. They witnessed an increase in questions each time the service was announced. Campus newspaper ads were found to be less effective (Kratzert, Richey, and Wasserman 2001, 80).

Particularly interesting to note from Table 2: KANAnswer was endorsed by the governor of Kansas (Stockham, Turtle, and Hansen 2002/2003, 261); at the University of Illinois, the library gained publicity through a campus newspaper article by promoting virtual reference in tandem with a term paper counseling service (Kibbee, Ward, and Ma 2002, 27).

WORD-OF-MOUTH

Numerous articles discuss the importance of "buy-in"–making sure that the vast majority of the librarians on staff want the new virtual reference service to succeed. As Girvin's marketing guidelines suggest, "reference librarians who serve users day-to-day have significant influence over the success of the program." The guidelines offer a number of tips for maintaining interest in and enthusiasm for virtual reference service (2002, 43-44).

The Illinois collaborative, MyWebLibrarian, emphasizes "your voice" and asks that participating librarians talk up the service with boards, committees, and user groups (Lindbloom 2003). At the University of Illinois, librarians from all units were kept informed about the development of their virtual reference service through faculty and staff meetings, and were invited to test the service prior to its implementation (Kibbee, Ward, and Ma 2002, 27). At Cal-State Fullerton and Saddleback College, the desire was that "all public service librarians should have a clear understanding of what type of service will be provided and to whom" (Kratzert, Richey, and Wasserman 2001, 79). With this core information, librarians could promote the service during library orientations, instruction sessions, and elsewhere on campus. Arizona wanted to ensure that its student workers could spread the word as well, and planned to keep them well-informed about virtual reference offerings (Bracke 2003).

Ronan devotes two pages to the topic of promotion through direct contact, and she echoes the theme of convincing both student and professional staff to continually market the service to patrons. "Encourage staff to promote your chat service to anyone who reveals they research at home . . . if you have chat service hours beyond those of your reference desk, put a recording on an answering machine and a sign at the reference desk directing users to the service . . . encourage student staff members working late hours to direct questions" (2003, 169). Librarians' informal networks of contacts on campus can also prove invaluable; in particular, subject liaisons can distribute literature to their faculty and ask to present the service at department meetings. Ronan has found the following approach to be effective: she identifies faculty with online syllabi, then sends each a personalized letter introducing the service, including scenarios in which the virtual librarian could assist students in the class (2003, 168).

CONCLUSIONS

The literature on marketing virtual reference services remains at an infant stage. Plenty has been written about initiating digital reference services, but frequently the marketing efforts associated with the startup garner no more than two paragraphs. However, recent books on virtual reference from Coffman, Meola and Stormont, and Ronan have each devoted a chapter solely to marketing, and the Girvin guidelines for marketing virtual reference may prove to be a turning point. Ideally, articles whose primary focus is marketing virtual reference will soon be published. The beginnings of such a movement can be spotted in the presentations by Bracke and Hirko at the 2003 Virtual Reference Desk Conference. Duncan's article from April 2004 is a good example of using focus group testing to find the best name for a virtual reference service.

Articles on the most effective promotional materials, the most receptive audiences, and the best web placement will hopefully also enter the literature soon. They would be a welcome addition, because so many accounts of the introduction of virtual reference reveal a common theme: users like the service, but the population of users is smaller than hoped. If the service itself is worthwhile and targeted toward an appropriate market, boosting usage may be just a matter of educating library users about how they can benefit by using virtual reference.

QUICK BIB

Bracke, Marianne. 2003. Dynamic Marketing to Targeted Markets. Presented at the Virtual Reference Desk Conference, San Antonio, Texas. http://www.vrd2003.org/proceedings/presentation.cfm?PID=179.

Girvin Strategic Branding & Design. 2002. King County Library System and University of Washington Virtual Reference Services: Marketing Guidelines. http://www.secstate.wa.gov/library/libraries/projects/virtualRef/textdocs/MarketingGuidelines.pdf.

Hirko, Buff. 2003. Bull's-eye! Targeting Virtual Patrons. Presented at the Virtual Reference Desk Conference, San Antonio, Texas. http://www.vrd2003.org/proceedings/presentation.cfm?PID=193.

REFERENCES

Association of Southeast Research Libraries. 2003. Project Proposal. http://www.aserl.org/projects/vref/ASERL%20vRef%20Service%20Proposal.final.pdf.

Barber, Peggy, and Linda Wallace. 2002. 10 Tips for Marketing Virtual Reference Services (VRS). http://www.ssdesign.com/librarypr/download/odds_and_ends/marketing_vps.pdf.

Blank, Phil. 2002/2003. Virtual Reference at Duke: An Informal History. *The Reference Librarian* 79/80: 215-24.

Bracke, Marianne. 2003. Dynamic Marketing to Targeted Markets. Presented at the Virtual Reference Desk Conference, San Antonio, Texas. http://www.vrd2003.org/proceedings/presentation.cfm?PID=179.

Coffman, Steve. 2003. *Going Live: Starting and Running a Virtual Reference Desk.* Chicago: American Library Association.

Coffman, Steve, and Linda Arret. 2004. To Chat or Not to Chat–Taking Yet Another Look at Virtual Reference, Part 2. *Searcher* 12 (August). http://www.infotoday.com/searcher/sep04/arret_coffman.shtml.

Coppola, Elaine, Tasha Cooper, Tom Keays, Sean MacMaster, Suzanne Preate, and Donna Sullivan. 2002. Web Chat Action Team Final Report and Recommendations. Syracuse University Library. http://libwww.syr.edu/information/strategicplan/progressreports/webchat/finalreport.pdf.

Duncan, Vicky, and Darlene M. Fichter. 2004. What Words and Where? Applying Usability Testing to Name a New Live Reference Service. *Journal of the Medical Library Association* 92: 218-25.

Girvin Strategic Branding & Design. 2002. *King County Library System and University of Washington Virtual Reference Services: Marketing Guidelines*. http://www. secstate.wa.gov/library/libraries/projects/virtualRef/textdocs/MarketingGuidelines.pdf.

Hirko, Buff. 2003. Bull's-eye! Targeting Virtual Patrons. Presented at the Virtual Reference Desk Conference, San Antonio, Texas. http://www.vrd2003.org/proceedings/presentation.cfm?PID=193.

Janes, Joseph. 2003. The Global Census of Digital Reference. Presented at the Virtual Reference Desk Conference, San Antonio, Texas. http://www.vrd2003.org/proceedings/presentation.cfm?PID=162.

Kawakami, Alice. 2002. Delivering Digital Reference. *Library Journal netConnect* 15 (April): 28-29. http://www.libraryjournal.com/article/CA210717.

Kibbee, Jo, David Ward, and Wei Ma. 2002. Virtual Service, Real Data: Results of a Pilot Study. *Reference Services Review* 30: 25-36.

Kratzert, Mona, Debora Richey, and Carol Wasserman. 2001. Tips and Snags of Cyberreference. *College and Undergraduate Libraries* 8: 73-82.

Lindbloom, Mary-Carol. 2003. Marketing Digital Reference Services. Presented to the meeting of the MOUSS Cooperative Reference Services Committee. http://www.ala. org/ala/rusa/rusaourassoc/rusasections/mouss/moussection/mousscomm/cooperativeref/lindbloom.ppt.

Maxwell, Nancy Kalikow. 2004. The Seven Deadly Sins of Library Technology. *American Libraries* 35 (September): 40-42.

Meola, Marc, and Sam Stormont. 2002. *Starting and Operating Live Virtual Reference Services: A How-To-Do-It Manual For Librarians*. New York: Neal-Schuman Publishers.

Ronan, Jana Smith. 2003. *Chat Reference: A Guide to Live Virtual Reference Services*. Westport, CT: Libraries Unlimited.

Sims, Melanie E. 2002/2003. Virtual Reference Services: The LSU Libraries Experience. *The Reference Librarian* 79/80: 267-79.

Sweet, Marianne F., David M. Lisa, and Dale E. Colston. 2003. Q and A NJ: Service Design and Impact. In *Virtual Reference Services: Issues and Trends*, 49-69. New York: The Haworth Information Press.

Stockham, Marcia, Elizabeth Turtle, and Eric Hansen. 2002/2003. KANAnswer: A Collaborative Statewide Virtual Reference Pilot Project. *The Reference Librarian* 79/80: 257-66.

Wells, Catherine A. 2003. Location, Location, Location: The Importance of Placement of the Chat Request Button. *Reference and User Services Quarterly* 43 (Winter): 133-37.

APPENDIX. Virtual Reference Web Sites

To review the virtual reference offerings from the libraries mentioned in this article, visit the following web sites:

Association of Southeastern Research Libraries (ASERL):
http://www.ask-a-librarian.org/

Cal Poly Pomona (CPP):
http://www.csupomona.edu/~library/html/ask_a_librarian.html

California State University, Fullerton (CSF): http://www.library.fullerton.edu/

Case Western Reserve University (Case):
http://library.case.edu/ksl/ref/ask.html

Duke University (Duke): http://www.lib.duke.edu/reference/refq.htm

Illinois state collaborative (Illinois): http://www.myweblibrarian.com/

Kansas state collaborative (Kansas): http://www.kananswer.org

Louisiana State University (LSU): http://www.lib.lsu.edu/virtual/

New Jersey state collaborative (NJ): http://www.qandanj.org/

Saddleback College (SC): http://www.saddleback.edu/AP/LR/?exp=/AP/LR/

Syracuse University (SU):
http://libwww.syr.edu/information/reference/index.html

University of Arizona (UA): http://www.library.arizona.edu/askalibrarian/

University of Illinois at Urbana-Champaign (UI):
http://web.library.uiuc.edu/ugl/vr/

Washington state collaborative (Wash):
http://www.secstate.wa.gov/library/libraries/projects/virtualRef/

Marketing Resources
for the Busy Librarian

Deborah O. Lee

SUMMARY. This article provides an overview of some of the most useful marketing resources, in print and online, available to librarians. Included are general introductory marketing guides, as well as books and articles on marketing specialized services such as library instruction or reference. Marketing advice from key library vendors, Internet sites, and resources for continuing education are also included. *[Article copies available for a fee from The Haworth Document Delivery Service: 1-800-HAWORTH. E-mail address: <docdelivery@haworthpress.com> Website: <http://www.HaworthPress.com> © 2005 by The Haworth Press, Inc. All rights reserved.]*

KEYWORDS. Marketing, outreach, public relations, publicity, bibliography, resources, continuing education

Deborah O. Lee (MLS, University of North Carolina-Chapel Hill; MSLS and PhD, Mississippi State University) is Associate Professor and Coordinator of Library Instructional Services, Corporate and Statistical Research Center, Mississippi State University Libraries, Mississippi State, MS 39762 (address e-mail to: dlee@library.msstate.edu).

[Haworth co-indexing entry note]: "Marketing Resources for the Busy Librarian." Lee, Deborah O. Co-published simultaneously in *College & Undergraduate Libraries* (The Haworth Information Press, an imprint of The Haworth Press, Inc.) Vol. 12, No. 1/2, 2005, pp. 81-91; and: *Real-Life Marketing and Promotion Strategies in College Libraries: Connecting with Campus and Community* (ed: Barbara Whitney Petruzzelli) The Haworth Information Press, an imprint of The Haworth Press, Inc., 2005, pp. 81-91. Single or multiple copies of this article are available for a fee from The Haworth Document Delivery Service [1-800-HAWORTH, 9:00 a.m. - 5:00 p.m. (EST). E-mail address: docdelivery@haworthpress.com].

doi:10.1300/J106v12n01_06

INTRODUCTION

Most academic librarians agree on the necessity of marketing library services. Whether we call it outreach, liaison work, or public relations, many of us have embraced the need to actively promote library resources and services. The professional literature has responded–the number of marketing resources continues to increase. New books, useful articles, and informative web resources appear frequently. Unfortunately, our day has not gotten any longer!

This bibliographic article provides an overview of some of the most useful resources available to librarians. No effort is made to provide a comprehensive bibliography of marketing citations. (Such a bibliography would be a book-length manuscript and would take much too long to read!) Rather, this article provides a selective, annotated listing of books, articles, and web sites to assist the busy librarian in staying current with developments in library marketing. The items selected provide valuable information and assistance to librarians as they develop marketing plans, conduct marketing research, and promote specialized services.

An amazing amount of information about library marketing has "sprung up" on the Internet. Librarians are never hesitant to share their experiences and suggestions, and the area of marketing is no exception. In addition, a number of vendors have also developed materials specifically designed to assist their customers (us!) in promoting library services. No bibliography of marketing resources would be complete without the inclusion of these web-based resources. However, an article with URLs is by its very nature problematic; by the time the article actually sees print, many of the URLs may be out-of-date. The URLs referenced in this article were accurate as of April 2005. To assist future readers, the author will maintain a listing of all web-based materials cited in this article and will attempt to keep the URLs up-to-date. This updated web site may be found at: http://www2.msstate.edu/marketing/.

GENERAL MARKETING GUIDES

A number of general or comprehensive marketing guides have been developed for librarians. These resources typically present the marketing process as a series of steps and provide advice for each step.

Brodsky, Karen. "If You Build It Will They Come? Using a New Library Building to Establish a Culture of Marketing." *Reference Librarian* 82 (2003): 183-197.

Brodsky recounts the efforts of the University Library at Sonoma State University to develop a comprehensive marketing plan. The unveiling of a new library building is used as the catalyst to develop marketing strategies. These strategies included the development of new programs and the reallocation of staff time to marketing duties.

Siess, Judith A. *The Visible Librarian: Asserting Your Value With Marketing and Advocacy.* Chicago: American Library Association, 2003. ISBN: 0-8389-0848-9.

Siess challenges librarians to raise their visibility, both to their users and their administrators or funding agencies. She argues that marketing strategies provide an excellent mechanism for raising both the librarian's and the library's visibility. She focuses on four distinct aspects of visibility: marketing, publicity, public relations, and most importantly, advocacy. Siess has thoroughly documented her work and has an extensive bibliography for those wishing to delve even deeper into the marketing literature!

Wallace, Linda K. *Libraries, Mission, & Marketing: Writing Mission Statements That Work.* Chicago, American Library Association, 2004. ISBN: 0-8389-0867-5.

This short work (82 pages) packs a powerful punch. Wallace shows how to use mission statements as a marketing tool. She provides tips and strategies for developing a mission statement with marketing goals in mind. At least half of the book is dedicated to providing actual examples from all types of libraries. Each entry includes the contact information for the library and its mission statement.

Walters, Suzanne. *Library Marketing That Works!* New York: Neal Schumann Publishers, 2004. ISBN: 1-55570-473-5.

Provides a detailed, step-by-step strategy for developing a comprehensive library marketing program. Unlike some other, more dated materials, this up-to-date work includes strategies for incorporating web pages and listservs into the marketing mix. Walters also presents a strong case for developing relationships with key stakeholders through the development of contact databases and specialized outreach activities. One unique feature of Walters' work is the accompanying CD-ROM, which includes reproducible handouts and worksheets, as well as materials for a "One-Day Marketing Workshop" including a PowerPoint presentation and handouts.

Weingand, Darlene E. *Future-Driven Library Marketing.* Chicago: American Library Association, 1998. ISBN: 0-8389-0735-0.

One of the classics in the library marketing literature, Weingand's 1998 work focuses on positioning the library as the information provider of choice for all library users. Weingand covers the foundations of marketing, including information on using the Delphi method to develop a "futures" screen. She expands on the 4 P's of marketing (product, price, place, and promotion) by adding prelude (defined as a marketing audit) and postlude (evaluation).

Weingand, Darlene. E. "Preparing for the new Millennium: The Case for Using Marketing Strategies." *Library Trends* 43 (Winter 1995): 295-317.

Darlene Weingand was one of the early writers to address customer service and marketing issues in libraries. This opening essay in a theme issue dedicated to marketing library issues does an excellent job of outlining basic concepts in marketing. In addition to providing an overview, Weingand lays out nine steps in the marketing process: planning, conducting the marketing audit, defining the library market, developing marketable goals and objectives, developing products, identifying costs, using channels of distribution, promotion, and evaluation. Each step is defined in terms of a library environment.

SPECIALIZED SERVICES

The following resources can assist libraries in promoting new services and resources, and in raising the visibility of existing resources.

Baker, Sharon L. and Karen L. Wallace. *The Responsive Public Library: How to Develop and Market a Winning Collection.* Englewood, CO: Libraries Unlimited, 2002. ISBN: 1-5630-8648-4.

Baker and Wallace's groundbreaking book, now in its second edition, is written for the public library market. This in no way, however, lessens its value for an academic library readership. I'm unaware of any text written for academic libraries that handles the concept of collection development from a marketing perspective. Libraries (regardless of type) typically spend the bulk of their non-personnel budget on electronic and print collections; incorporating this aspect of library operations into a marketing strategy benefits both the library and the end user. Many aspects of sound collection development, such as a community needs analysis, closely mirrors marketing research. Baker and Wallace provide an excellent primer for both collection development and marketing.

Cruickshank, John and David Nowak. "Marketing Reference Resources and Services Through a University Outreach Program." *The Reference Librarian* 73 (2001): 265-280.

Cruickshank and Nowak discuss the impact on reference services of a library's outreach program. The outreach program at Mississippi State University Libraries involved close collaboration between a selected liaison from the library and faculty in various academic departments. The authors show the relationship between a library-wide outreach initiative and the ability to successfully market reference services.

Harrington, Deborah Lynn and Xiaodong Li. "Spinning an Academic Web Community: Measuring Marketing Effectiveness." *Journal of Academic Librarianship* 27 (May 2001): 199-207.

Harrington and Li report on efforts to promote chat sessions and engagement of users in an academic virtual library community (VLC). The authors surveyed participants and found that sustained marketing efforts were needed to promote the VLC. Direct e-mail efforts and networking through one-on-one professional relationships were the two most effective means of developing the VLC.

Jacso, Peter. "Promoting the Library by Using Technology." *Computers in Libraries* 21 (September 2001): 58-60.

Jacso discusses ways to use technology to promote library acquisitions and to streamline interlibrary loan activities. Web-based wish lists, new acquisitions lists, and purchase request forms can assist libraries in promoting technical service activities.

Kirkendall, Carolyn A. (ed.) *Marketing Instructional Services: Applying Private Sector Techniques to Plan and Promote Bibliographic Instruction.* Ann Arbor, MI: Pierian Press, 1986. ISBN: 0-87650-201-X.

Although dated, this volume provides papers presented at the 13th LOEX Library Instruction Conference, held at Eastern Michigan University in 1984. The focus for the conference was marketing library instructional services and most papers deal with some aspect of marketing and promotion.

Nims, Julia K. "Marketing Library Instruction Services: Changes and Trends." *Reference Services Review* 27 (1999): 249-253.

Nims updates topics from the 13th LOEX Library Instruction Conference (see Kirkendall above). The author discusses the role of marketing and publicity/promotion in the development of successful library instructional services.

VENDOR RESOURCES

Companies who serve the library market recognize the increasing value of marketing for their customers–librarians! A number of vendors have applied their professional expertise to develop instructional materials specifically designed to assist librarians in promoting their resources and services. The following resources are freely available online.

In addition to teaching librarians the fundamentals of marketing, many vendors can also supply promotional materials to assist you in raising the visibility of their specific services or databases. In the past, I've received t-shirts, pens, balloons, flyers, posters, user guides, and even a laptop computer case. Often, all it takes is a call to your local account representative. These promotional materials are professionally designed and ready for distribution, helping the busy librarian enhance both instructional and marketing efforts.

3M Library Systems: *Strategic Marketing for Academic and Research Libraries.* Available online at: http://cms.3m.com/cms/US/en/2-115/czrRzFZ/view.jhtml.

This web site provides training materials and PowerPoint slides from a recent presentation on marketing at the American Library Association's annual meeting. Materials include manuals (as pdf files) for facilitators and participants, allowing libraries to use these materials for in-house training and as a source of marketing-related ideas and information.

Factiva: *Factiva InfoPro Resource Center.* Available online at: http://www.factiva.com/infopro/resource.asp.

Developed by Dow Jones & Reuter's Factiva service, this web site includes resources to assist with the development of strategic plans, formulating marketing goals, and promoting library resources. While the primary focus is on corporate information centers and special libraries, much of the material available applies equally well to academic libraries, regardless of size.

Thomson Gale: *Academic Library Promotions.* Available online at: http://www.galegroup.com/free_resources/marketing/academic/index. htm.

Gale Group offers a variety of promotional and marketing resources for libraries, most of which are not database or vendor specific. Everything from reproducible bookmarks and posters to templates for press releases can be found on their web site. Materials are available for academic libraries as well as special law or health science libraries. Spanish language materials are also available.

LexisNexis: *Marketing tips for Information Professionals.* Available online at: http://www.lexisnexis.com/infopro/training/reference/pdf/ MarketingTips.pdf.

LexisNexis provides an online (pdf) guide to marketing for information professionals. This 32-page guide includes an overview of the marketing process as well as exercises that the librarian can use to develop marketing strategies for his or her own library.

INTERNET RESOURCES

Brand Aid: Selected Resources. Available online at: http://www.ala. org/ala/rusa/rusaourassoc/rusasections/brass/brassprotools/brasspres/ marketing/brandaidselected.htm.

(Note: ALA's URLs are notoriously long and often break when you try to copy them into a browser. This resource can be found under RUSA's BRASS section of professional tools.)

Developed from a presentation by the same name in 2002, this online listing of articles, books, and web sites can assist anyone wanting to learn more about marketing library services. Developed by Shelley Bennett of the Chicago Public Library and Mary Gilles of Washington State University, the bibliography covers materials of interest to both public and academic libraries. The bibliography has not been updated since 2002, so other sources must be consulted for more recent publications. But even though dated, it provides a good overview of the applied literature in the area of marketing library services.

Marketing @ your library. Available online at: http://www.ala.org/ala/acrl/acrlissues/marketingyourlib/marketingyour.htm.

Developed by ACRL as part of ALA's Campaign for America's Libraries, this web site provides access to the @ your library Toolkit for Academic and Research Libraries, which was produced in 2003. Other resources available include clip art and graphics for use in promotional materials (located under the "Academic and Research Library Campaign" link), information about related ACRL and ALA discussion lists, and updates on ACRL's advertising campaign. The online toolkit, available as a pdf file, provides useful quotes and strategies for marketing academic libraries.

Marketing Ideas for Libraries. Available online at: http://www.owls.lib.wi.us/info/desks/bc/imarket/default.htm.

This web site is maintained by Beth Carpenter of the Outagamie Waupaca Library System. It provides access to bibliographies and links of interest, as well as short articles on various aspects of marketing library services. A very useful section contains ideas for online activities and services that promote library use.

Marketing Our Libraries: On and Off the Internet. Available online at: http://www.librarysupportstaff.com/marketinglibs.html.

This web site provides information concerning workshops, recent publications, and links to other web sites related to the areas of publicity and marketing library services. Developed and maintained by Mary Niederlander, a library technician who worked at the Hospital Medical Library in Buffalo, New York until her retirement in January of 2005. Niederlander has developed a site that pulls together information for library professionals and staff, including a comprehensive marketing section. While the organizational structure can be confusing, this content-rich site provides citations not easily found in other online sources.

Marketing: Sources for Marketing Information and Library Services. Available online at: http://dis.shef.ac.uk/sheila/marketing/sources. htm.

This marketing meta site was developed by Sheila Webber, a lecturer in the Department of Information Studies at the University of Sheffield. While the web page does not appear to have had content added to it since November 2002, most of the links continue to work. This online bibliography identifies conference proceedings and journal articles in the area of library marketing resources and is integrated into Webber's other marketing web sites.

Marketing the Library. Available online at: http://www.olc.org/marketing/.

Developed by the Ohio Library Corporation (OLC), this web-based resource is developed for public library staff. The self-paced modules provide staff with a general overview of the marketing process and includes quizzes and links to external sources. While specifically designed for the public library sector, much of the material is equally applicable for an academic environment.

CONTINUING EDUCATION

Once you make the commitment to pursuing marketing strategies in your library, where do you go for continued support and ideas? The discussion lists and journals listed below are some of the options available for continuing education in the area of library marketing.

@Your Library E-mail List (Campaign for America's Libraries)

Developed as part of the American Library Association's Campaign for America's Libraries, this e-mail listserv offers participants the ability to share promotional activities and to network with other librarians in the use of ALA's "@ your library" promotional materials. To subscribe, send an e-mail to subscribe-campaign@ala.org. Subscribers should receive a confirmation within twenty-four hours. For additional information about the "@ your library" campaign, see ALA's web site: http://www.ala.org/ala/pio/campaign/campaignamericas.htm.

AcademicPR

Developed by the Association of College and Research Libraries (ACRL), in collaboration with ALA's Campaign for America's Libraries, this listserv provides academic and research librarians a forum for discussion of promotional and marketing activities. To subscribe, send a message to listproc@ala.org with the message: subscribe ACADEMICPR First-name Last-name.

MLS: Marketing Library Services

The only journal or newsletter solely dedicated to marketing issues in libraries, MLS is published six times a year by Information Today. Issues typically include articles, short reviews of books, and ideas for promotional activities. Articles cover all types of libraries. The newsletter maintains a web page at: http://www.infotoday.com/mls/default.shtml. While the newsletter is not available online, typically one article per issue is freely available on the web.

Marketing Treasures. Available online at: http://www.chrisolson.com/marketingtreasures/indexmt.html.

This online newsletter is developed and maintained by Chris Olson & Associates, a marketing management firm focused on the library market. Issues typically contain articles reporting on library marketing activities, book reviews, and advice for developing successful promotional materials. The newsletter migrated to electronic format in January 2005. Back issues are available on the web site, and readers may register to receive future issues.

PR Talk

Maintained by ALA, this e-mail list includes promotional ideas for ALA-sponsored events and other topics related to publicity in libraries. For additional information, to search the archives, or subscription information, see: http://www.ala.org/ala/pio/electronicdiscussion/electronicdiscussion.htm.

CONCLUSION

The marketing literature for librarians continues to be robust, with new resources appearing in both print and on the Internet on a regular basis. Public and special libraries have dealt with the need to raise the visibility of their organizations for a long time. Academic libraries are now following suit, turning to the concepts found in marketing to more forcefully articulate their role on the university or college campus. Marketing helps us connect with our users and to develop services and collections that meet their needs. This article has attempted to illustrate some of the many resources librarians have at their disposal when exploring issues of marketing. Few of us can spend forty hours a week dedicated solely to marketing issues. But with the resources listed above, we can learn the basics of marketing library services and incorporate marketing concepts into our collection development, outreach, instruction, and even management activities.

Drop Them a Postcard:
Another Way to Reach Your Patrons

John A. Cosgrove

SUMMARY. In the Lucy Scribner Library at Skidmore College, we have produced 11 different postcards to promote services and collections. We have discovered the advantages as well as the limitations of using postcards as marketing/instructional/informational tools. There have also been some practical lessons to be learned along the way. *[Article copies available for a fee from The Haworth Document Delivery Service: 1-800-HAWORTH. E-mail address: <docdelivery@haworthpress.com> Website: <http://www.HaworthPress.com> © 2005 by The Haworth Press, Inc. All rights reserved.]*

KEYWORDS. College libraries, marketing, postcards

Seeking an alternative to the traditional 8 1/2" × 11" handout at the Lucy Scribner Library at Skidmore College, a private liberal arts college of approximately 2,300 students located near the Adirondack region of upstate New York, we created a postcard in fall 2001 to promote

John A. Cosgrove (BA, English, SUNY College at Oneonta; MA, English, University at Albany; MLS, University at Albany) is Access Services/Humanities Librarian, Skidmore College, 815 North Broadway, Saratoga Springs, NY 12866-1632 (address e-mail to: jcosgrov@skidmore.edu).

[Haworth co-indexing entry note]: "Drop Them a Postcard: Another Way to Reach Your Patrons." Cosgrove, John A. Co-published simultaneously in *College & Undergraduate Libraries* (The Haworth Information Press, an imprint of The Haworth Press, Inc.) Vol. 12, No. 1/2, 2005, pp. 93-100; and: *Real-Life Marketing and Promotion Strategies in College Libraries: Connecting with Campus and Community* (ed: Barbara Whitney Petruzzelli) The Haworth Information Press, an imprint of The Haworth Press, Inc., 2005, pp. 93-100. Single or multiple copies of this article are available for a fee from The Haworth Document Delivery Service [1-800-HAWORTH, 9:00 a.m. - 5:00 p.m. (EST). E-mail address: docdelivery@haworthpress.com].

Available online at http://www.haworthpress.com/web/CUL
© 2005 by The Haworth Press, Inc. All rights reserved.
doi:10.1300/J106v12n01_07

a new online self-renewal service. Within a year, our postcards evolved from campus-printed, single-color, hand-trimmed cards on lightweight card stock to full-color, retail-quality cards printed on standard postcard stock by a commercial printer. The postcards describe a range of library services (e.g., online interlibrary loan requests) and collections (e.g., visual resources and special collections). They are formatted like traditional tourist postcards. Image and text are on the front, and, except for a caption and the library name, address, and URL, there is plenty of white space to write on the back. The backs even have the standard vertical line in the middle to separate address space from note space.

The postcards are conspicuously displayed on a rack at the main entrance of the library and are available to our students, faculty, and staff, as well as the many potential students and their families who visit during admissions tours. They have been distributed in instruction sessions for our own students and in occasional sessions for visiting middle- and high-school classes, included in orientation packets for new faculty, and mailed to Friends of the Library.

It is tempting to call our effort a postcard campaign—we produced ten different postcards, with print runs of 500 each, in less than a year—but it is more accurate to call it a postcard experiment. We did not develop a formal plan. We produced the first postcard and were happy with the results. What started out as a simple attempt to get the attention of our patrons turned into library-wide effort. Several of the postcards were created out of the enthusiasm generated by having successfully produced first one, and then another and then another. This was especially true once we switched to a commercial printer and produced the kind of postcards that we had envisioned at the outset: postcards physically (if not graphically) equal to the kind you might purchase in a tourist shop. At that point, every department in the library wanted a postcard and we consciously made sure each produced one.

When I first proposed creating a postcard, I thought of it as a novel alternative to the standard instructional or informational handouts. Aside from using different colored paper, handouts all seemed very much the same. We wanted to try something different. We also wanted to have something physical to hand to our patrons, as most of our handouts had migrated to the Web.

Of the first ten postcards we produced, four of the postcards might be characterized as promotional/instructional: "Self-Renewal Procedure," "Online Interlibrary Loan (ILL) Service," "Search the Library by Subject," and "Requesting Materials for the Library." (The first three of these were new initiatives.) The remaining six postcards are promotional/informational. They describe particular collections (Curriculum Library, Special Collections, U.S. Government Documents, Visual Resources) or services (Instruction Services, Reference Services).

In hindsight, not all of the postcards were equally successful. However, we learned something with each of them, and, with the benefit of that same hindsight, the pros and cons of the postcard as a marketing and instructional tool are easier to discern. We also learned, via simple trial and error, the practical aspects of postcard production. Perhaps some of the lessons we learned will allow your postcard experience to be more campaign than experiment.

FORMAT

It is important to point out that postcards cannot replace all handouts. To the extent that you can work the necessary text onto a 4 1/4″ × 6″ space (along with graphics), postcards can do the job of an 8 1/2″× 11″ handout. But handouts dealing with complex topics that require a great deal of text, such as how to conduct research in a subject area, just won't work in this format.

FUNCTION

As we designed the first postcard, it became apparent that not only is a postcard physically different from a handout, but its primary function is also different. The primary function of a postcard is to promote, rather than to instruct. Our first postcard promoted the use of our new online renewal option. (See Figure 1.) We searched the college yearbooks hoping to find a "retro" photograph that our students could identify with. We chose a black-and-white, 1968 Skidmore College Yearbook photo of a student reading under a tree to depict the concept of self-renewal. Conveniently, the instructions fit on the postcard in a legible font size and did not overwhelm the photograph. The postcard was primarily promoting this new service. The actual instructions, although important, were secondary.

In contrast, the Web page for the new service, although it used the same photo, background color, and text as the postcard, was more like a traditional handout. Its primary aim was instructing patrons on how to use the service. The text was more prominent, set in a larger font and po-

FIGURE 1. Postcard for Online Renewal Option

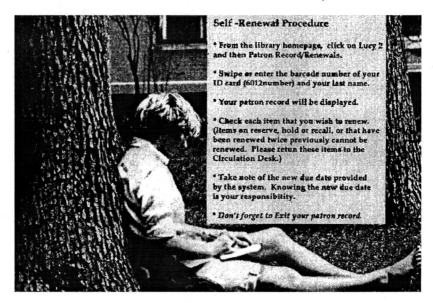

Self-Renewal Procedure

* From the library homepage, click on Lucy 2 and then Patron Record/Renewals.

* Swipe or enter the barcode number of your ID card (6012number) and your last name.

* Your patron record will be displayed.

* Check each item that you wish to renew. (Items on reserve, hold or recall, or that have been renewed twice previously cannot be renewed. Please retun these items to the Circulation Desk.)

* Take note of the new due date provided by the system. Knowing the new due date is your responsibility.

* *Don't forget to Exit your patron record.*

sitioned next to the image, rather than inset. The page itself was positioned in the library catalog so that patrons had to go through it before proceeding to the self-renewal log-in screen.

GRAPHICS

Another important distinction between postcards and handouts is that postcards are primarily visual, not textual. Select your images carefully to avoid choosing form over substance, an issue we grappled with.

Like the first postcard, the second promoted a new online resource. We had just moved from print to Web-based request forms for interlibrary loan and we wanted to tell the campus about it. The postcard also instructed the patron in how to use the new forms. The image used on our postcard for online interlibrary loan was a yearbook photo of a student working at a table between walls covered with periodical shelves. It was chosen primarily because our first postcard used a yearbook photo successfully. Unlike the image on the first postcard, the image on the second postcard bore little relation to the subject of the card. We choose an image because of the yearbook theme, rather than because it illustrated the content of the card.

We probably made a similar mistake when we created a postcard on using a subject approach to searching the library's online resources. A colleague created a supersaturated purple negative image of the library, which we loved. We hoped that the strong image would attract patrons on its own. It did. However, an image more illustrative of that postcard's topic would probably have been more effective in conveying the message.

Based on the number of postcards that we have left, these two postcards are no less popular than any of the other cards. However, upon reflection, images that are interesting, yet somehow connected to the message of the postcard are superior to images that are simply interesting. Grabbing the patron's attention is wonderful, but your message should be not be lost in the process.

SOFTWARE

Since the postcard is a visual medium, you will need to use a graphics program to manipulate images, color, and text. We used Adobe PhotoShop and were lucky enough to have at least three staff members who were fluent enough with the program to work on layouts. Media or computer services on your campus might be able to provide your staff with training in graphics software if needed.

EDITING

It is probably a good idea to establish a formal editorial structure from the outset of the project. We used a distributed approach in the initial writing and design, with members of different departments working on their own postcards, a few individuals acting as informal editors, and the College Librarian as the publisher, having final say. Unfortunately, in at least one case an individual developed a postcard outside of this informal structure and was surprised by the considerable revisions that were imposed before the postcard was approved for printing. Adopting a more official editorial procedure may alleviate hurt feelings, not to mention saving time and energy.

COST

Another consideration is cost. The campus print shop printed 500 postcards for $125, while a commercial printer charged $137 for the same number. The cost of printing 500 handouts, even double-sided on colored paper, is minimal in comparison.

PRINTING

As mentioned previously, our first three postcards were printed by our campus print shop. Unfortunately, the shop was not equipped to produce commercial quality postcards. The card stock was much thinner than traditional postcards, the finish was matte instead of glossy, and the first batch were larger than we specified and had to be trimmed by hand (by some very patient student workers) in order to actually be used as postcards. We later found a commercial printer who specializes in postcards and, for $12 more per 500, we got exactly what we were looking for–the kind of postcards you would find in a store. If your campus print shop is not capable of printing the kind of postcards that you want, and you are permitted to use a commercial printer, do it. It is likely that the cost will be comparable.

PRACTICAL USE

One of the benefits of postcards is their inherent ability to be mailed. This gives them a practical use beyond their in-house promotional/instructional/informational intent. We don't know how many of our postcards have actually been mailed by our patrons. However, we do know that we have been successful in producing something that can be mailed by us. In addition to general mailings to Friends of the Library, as a way to keep them informed about what we are doing, the Special Collections postcard was used as announcement card for a lecture by a visiting book artist. We had the campus print shop print the announcement on the back of the postcards and mailed them as invitations.

Overall, we found the postcard project to be successful. It was well-received by our patrons. Five hundred of each card was printed and, after two years, we are hard pressed to find some of them. Still, there were important lessons to be learned in our marketing experiment, and we tried to apply what we learned when we designed our eleventh postcard in 2004. (See Figure 2.)

This postcard promotes our new electronic reserves system. The graphic is a variation of the logo developed for the log-in page of the system. It is a visually interesting image (especially in color) and graphically represents how the system ties together different types of reserves (open, closed, and electronic reserves) and the patrons using the system (faculty and students). The text is descriptive, but concise. The goal was to get patrons to visit the URL at the top of the postcard, not to explain how to use the system. Details and instructions are available on the reserves Web pages.

The postcard was distributed to all of the faculty mailboxes just as we launched the new system. Along with an e-mail to faculty, the postcard was our main publicity effort for the new system. It seemed to work. We received a fair number of faculty inquiries about the new system. Some even tried it!

FIGURE 2. Electronic Reserves Postcard

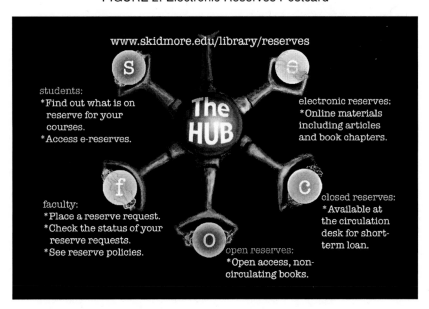

www.skidmore.edu/library/reserves

students:
*Find out what is on reserve for your courses.
*Access e-reserves.

The HUB

electronic reserves:
*Online materials including articles and book chapters.

faculty:
*Place a reserve request.
*Check the status of your reserve requests.
*See reserve policies.

closed reserves:
*Available at the circulation desk for short-term loan.

open reserves:
*Open access, non-circulating books.

QUICK BIB

Allen, Susan M. "Designing Library Handouts: Principles and Procedures." *Research Strategies* 11 (Winter 1993) 14-23.

Clark, Brenda J. and Jeanne M. Drewes. "Effective Graphics for Displays and Handouts." *Promoting Preservation Awareness in Libraries.* Edited by Jeanne M. Drewes and Julie A. Page. Westport, Connecticut: Greenwood Press, 1997. 313-328.

Maxymuck, John. *Using Desktop Publishing to Create Newsletters, Handouts, and Web Pages: A How-To-Do-It Manual.* New York: Neal-Schuman, 1997.

REFERENCES

Allen, Susan M. "Designing Library Handouts: Principles and Procedures." *Research Strategies* 11 (Winter 1993) 14-23.

Benedetti, Wendell. "Creating Postcards Digitally." *Petersen's Photographic.* Oct. 2000: D16-17.

Cho, Minnie. Postcard Graphics: *The Best Advertising and Promotional Design.* Rockport, Massachusetts: Rockport Publishers, 1997.

Clark, Brenda J. and Jeanne M. Drewes. "Effective Graphics for Displays and Handouts." *Promoting Preservation Awareness in Libraries.* Edited by Jeanne M. Drewes and Julie A. Page. Westport, Connecticut: Greenwood Press, 1997. 313-328.

Maxymuck, John. *Using Desktop Publishing to Create Newsletters, Handouts, and Web Pages: A How-To-Do-It Manual.* New York: Neal-Schuman, 1997.

Nichols, Michelle. "The Power of a Simple Postcard." *Business Week Online.* 3 Sept. 2002. *Academic Search Premier.* EBSCOHost. <http://search.epnet.com>.

Turner, Jim. "The Postcard: A Quick, Economical Way to Send a Message." *ABA Bank Marketing.* 1 Sep. 2004: 48. *ABI/INFORM Global.* ProQuest. <http://www.proquest.com/>.

Frankenstein @ *Our* Library–
Monstrous Opportunities for Marketing

Barbara M. MacAlpine

SUMMARY. When the Coates Library received notification that the ALA Traveling Exhibition on Frankenstein would be visiting Trinity University, staff reacted with excitement but also with a twinge of fear about all the effort entailed in developing programs and creating a major publicity campaign. This article focuses on the challenges the exhibit presented: who to turn to for help; how to involve members of the campus community; what to use for effective publicity; how to balance education and entertainment in the programs and their advertising; where to seek funds; and how to present three weeks of programming without exhausting the planners or overwhelming potential audiences. *[Article copies available for a fee from The Haworth Document Delivery Service: 1-800-HAWORTH. E-mail address: <docdelivery@haworthpress.com> Website: <http://www.HaworthPress.com> © 2005 by The Haworth Press, Inc. All rights reserved.]*

KEYWORDS. Traveling exhibits, marketing, academic libraries, Frankenstein, @ your library

Barbara M. MacAlpine (MLS, University of Wisconsin–Madison) is Science Librarian, Coates Library, Trinity University, One Trinity Place, San Antonio, TX 78212-7200 (address e-mail to: bmacalpi@trinity.edu).

[Haworth co-indexing entry note]: "Frankenstein @ *Our* Library–Monstrous Opportunities for Marketing." MacAlpine, Barbara M. Co-published simultaneously in *College & Undergraduate Libraries* (The Haworth Information Press, an imprint of The Haworth Press, Inc.) Vol. 12, No. 1/2, 2005, pp. 101-117; and: *Real-Life Marketing and Promotion Strategies in College Libraries: Connecting with Campus and Community* (ed: Barbara Whitney Petruzzelli) The Haworth Information Press, an imprint of The Haworth Press, Inc., 2005, pp. 101-117. Single or multiple copies of this article are available for a fee from The Haworth Document Delivery Service [1-800-HAWORTH, 9:00 a.m. - 5:00 p.m. (EST). E-mail address: docdelivery@ haworthpress.com].

WHY ASK FOR A MONSTER?

Trinity University's Coates Library was one of only 82 U.S. libraries selected by the American Library Association (ALA) to host the traveling exhibition "Frankenstein: Penetrating the Secrets of Nature" between 2002 and 2006. Developed by the National Library of Medicine (NLM) in collaboration with ALA, the traveling exhibit was based on a major exhibition produced by NLM in 1997-98. A series of six large, free-standing panels examined Mary Shelley and *Frankenstein* from a variety of viewpoints: literary, historical, scientific, medical, and societal. Tying it all together was the repeated use of an image of Frankenstein's Monster created by Universal Studios, a frightening face in glowing, gruesome shades of green.

Why would Trinity want the Frankenstein exhibit on its campus? As a small liberal arts college located three miles from the downtown area of a major city, Trinity might more likely display material that reflected the Alamo influence of its San Antonio home in South Texas. However, initial interest resulted from a First Year (freshman) Seminar entitled "Gods, Monsters, and Scientists," taught annually by faculty in the humanities, sciences, and engineering. In 2001, students in the three sections of the seminar came together early in the semester for an introduction to print resources by one of the Coates reference librarians. Later in the semester, while the students were reading Mary Shelley's famous work, the science librarian presented a class session on evaluating web sites, using Frankenstein as the topic. Thus, a direct tie-in to the curriculum already existed.

With academic interest in the subject matter established, the next step was to "sell" the idea of hosting the exhibit to the library director. Fortunately, the director agreed with Bjorncrantz, Garrett, and Hughes that "Unless libraries undertake special efforts to present themselves as cultural and intellectual leaders in their communities–and to be these leaders–they are often lumped together with other community services that are appreciated, but otherwise little noticed" (Bjorncrantz, Garrett, and Hughes 2000, 50). Library use at Trinity had declined significantly during the 1990s, to a door count low of 262,000 in the 2000-2001 fiscal year. Coates Library had lost its central role on campus (its "community" in this case). We believed that the Frankenstein exhibit could help push the pendulum in the other direction and show that the library was truly an "alive" and happening place.

While writing the proposal to host the exhibition, librarians learned that the same grant was also being sought by the University of Texas

Health Science Center–San Antonio (UTHSCSA), an institution of 2,750 students located 10 miles away on the northwest side of the city. Already concerned that Trinity, with a student body of less than 2,500, might be an unlikely selection, and faced with the probability that neither venue would be accepted, the two libraries developed a joint proposal in which each library would host the exhibit for half of the six-week tour. In retrospect, this was a propitious decision. Three weeks of Frankenstein on a small campus was exciting; six weeks could have become tedious.

WHERE TO START

As Mitchell and Zwemer pointed out when UCLA's College Library hosted an ALA-Smithsonian traveling exhibition, public libraries are more accustomed to community outreach and public programming than their academic counterparts (Mitchell and Zwemer 1999, 189). This assertion certainly held true at Trinity. Coates Library had no Exhibits Committee, no specific budget for marketing or programs, and no staff with experience in putting on a "really big show." ALA recognized that not all libraries have extensive backgrounds in these areas, and its Public Programs Office staff provided a very helpful three-day workshop that brought librarians together from each of the sites selected to host the exhibit. Trinity's science librarian returned from the 2002 Bethesda workshop with a large binder of information and suggestions (*Frankenstein Site Support Notebook*, 2002). By this time, the library had just eight months to prepare for the February 2003 exhibit.

The first challenge was to develop programming ideas, particularly for events that would satisfy ALA's requirements to have an opening reception for the public and to host a program on Mary Shelley and her book, *Frankenstein*. Because the exhibit would take place when First Year Seminar students would be reading *Frankenstein*, the lead seminar professor served as a sounding board and also provided invaluable suggestions. He recommended that we approach a faculty member in Modern Languages and Literatures who used *Frankenstein* as a text in one of her classes. She agreed to develop and present a public lecture on the topic "Frankenstein's Body: A Horror Story of Sex, Reproduction, and Social Responsibility." The librarians as a whole decided that a costume party was a fun and fitting theme for the opening reception that would follow this lecture. Other programming included two additional public lectures, a panel on cloning, a Frankenstein film festival, a blood drive, an art exhibit, and poster sessions created by Trinity students on topics that related to some aspect of the exhibition. The "February Frankenfest" was a packed three weeks, with enough activities to satisfy even the most ardent Frankenstein fan.

WHO WILL HELP?

From the beginning, it was obvious that outreach was essential, both to attract attendees to the exhibit and to request help with programming and advertising. Many campus groups and individuals were contacted, with functions as varied as the public relations office, a sorority (to run the blood drive), and the head of costumes in the speech and drama department. Most responded positively. Communications included great quantities of e-mail messages, contacts in person or over the phone, and web pages for more general information. With a theme like Frankenstein, we could be creative in appealing for help: from a web page announcing "Students–We Want Your Body (of Work)" (see Figure 1); to an e-mail with the subject line "Will You Support Frankenstein?" asking departmental chairs for contributions toward the cost of bringing a speaker to campus; and a challenge to "Enter If You Dare" (for contributions to the art exhibit) on our web site.

Working on the assumption that people would want to help, all communication was couched in terms of how much (money, time, expertise, or effort) prospective supporters would contribute, rather than giving them an option to say no. Support flowed in: from departments and individual faculty members, student groups and classes, the public relations office, instructional media services, the conferences and special programs office, food service, the President's office–even the University Chaplain. Faculty members agreed to serve on a panel or to encourage their students to participate in Frankenstein activities. The public relations staff offered all kinds of advice in addition to considerable free advertising. Food service personnel researched ideas to create particularly imaginative refreshments for the opening night reception. Moreover, the relationships we developed during the Frankenstein event have remained strong, so the project served as a very effective public relations tool.

GETTING THE WORD OUT

Serious publicity started on campus in December on the library web site. A link was added to the home page in a very prominent position,

FIGURE 1. Web Page Inviting Student Participation

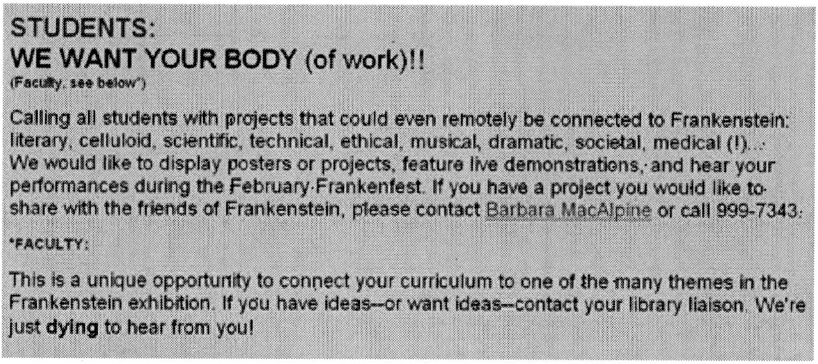

STUDENTS:
WE WANT YOUR BODY (of work)!!
(Faculty, see below")

Calling all students with projects that could even remotely be connected to Frankenstein: literary, celluloid, scientific, technical, ethical, musical, dramatic, societal, medical (!)... We would like to display posters or projects, feature live demonstrations, and hear your performances during the February Frankenfest. If you have a project you would like to share with the friends of Frankenstein, please contact Barbara MacAlpine or call 999-7343.

*FACULTY:

This is a unique opportunity to connect your curriculum to one of the many themes in the Frankenstein exhibition. If you have ideas—or want ideas—contact your library liaison. We're just **dying** to hear from you!

and a whole series of web pages (see Figure 2) were developed to promote individual programs and provide book and film bibliographies. On a more whimsical note, the library home page began sporting a small green face in varying locations (see Figure 3). Some staff feared that a hacker had altered the site, but eventually they realized that the face belonged to the figure on many of the Frankenstein pages, and that he was there by invitation. While the main link was removed after the exhibit left Trinity, pages may still be viewed at http://lib.trinity.edu/frank/.

Trinity met the challenge of getting high-quality printed publicity materials by partnering with a local business. A librarian's friend ran a graphic arts business and agreed to design and print posters, flyers, and table tents at a significant discount. In exchange, we agreed to add his logo to these pieces. Since all major events had separate advertising, he created more than a dozen individual pieces, most of which were reproduced in quantities of 100 or more. Copies of the main flyer were slid under the door of all dormitory rooms by a faithful cadre of student workers, and posters appeared on bulletin boards across campus (see Figure 4). While most printed publicity was distributed on campus, the library also supplied flyers to all public library branches and major bookstores in the area, and took posters to nearby colleges and universities.

Although the Trinity community was our primary audience, we also had an obligation–and desire–to promote the exhibit to the greater San Antonio area. One of the advantages of working within a college orga-

FIGURE 2. Frankenstein Home Page (http:/lib.trinity.edu/frank/)

nization is that it already has a knowledgeable and experienced public relations unit in place; the trick was to tap into it. Early in our planning, the "fearless" science librarian (as she was labeled by other library staff) visited the public relations office, described the coming exhibition in glowing terms, and asked for advertising advice. Perhaps because the Frankenstein concept had instant recognition and appeal, the Trinity public relations staff was particularly helpful in promoting the exhibit and our programs beyond the campus. They sent out a news release to local television and radio stations and newspapers, other higher education institutions, all of the city's high schools, educational organizations, area alumni, and local elected officials. Their glossy brochure advertising Trinity's calendar of events for the Spring 2003 semester included the major Frankenstein events. The university web site, which their staff maintains, prominently displayed a link to exhibit information on its home page, promoting awareness both on campus and off.

FIGURE 3. Coates Library's Home Page Took on a New "Face" as Frankenstein Time Approached

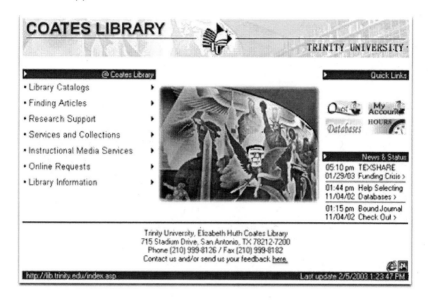

THE EDUCATIONAL COMPONENT

What were the goals associated with welcoming Frankenstein to the Coates Library? As Dutka, Hayes and Parnell have pointed out, exhibits can be an important teaching tool (Dutka, Hayes and Parnell 2002, 19). Thus, one objective was to offer visitors the opportunity for a quality independent learning experience. The exhibit was intended to support the First Year Seminar curriculum, as well. Peripherally, librarians hoped that Frankenstein would attract more people into the library and perhaps increase use of the collection. However, the primary goal for Trinity was to use the exhibit as a focal point for a range of enriching educational activities.

In addition to the public lecture on opening night, two outside speakers were brought in to discuss other aspects of the Frankenstein phenomenon. Dr. Timothy Marshall, author of *Murdering to Dissect: Grave Robbing, Frankenstein and the Anatomy Literature*, was identified through our close perusal of the bibliography in Jon Turney's book

FIGURE 4. Calendar of Horrible Happenings

(Calendar courtesy of Charles Chapman. Frankenstin image courtesy of Ronald V. Borst/Hollywood Movie Posters and Universal Studios Licensing, Inc.)

Frankenstein's Footsteps. He was contacted persistently by the lead First Year Seminar professor until we finally reached an agreement to have him visit the United States. Dr. Marshall came from East Anglia University in Great Britain to talk about concepts in his book. On the final evening of Frankenfest, Trinity hosted Dr. Susan Lederer, faculty member at Yale University and curator of the exhibition, who spoke on "Mary Shelley's Monster and Medical Science." She had presented at the Frankenstein workshop provided by the ALA Public Programs Office for exhibition hosts, where she indicated her willingness to speak at some of the exhibit sites. We were fortunate enough to persuade her that San Antonio in February might be a welcome change from Connecticut. In addition to their public lectures, both Dr. Marshall and Dr. Lederer also met with the First Year Seminar class, where they spoke on related topics and answered students' questions. After their visits to Trinity, the two speakers appeared at UTHSCSA in order to share expenses and coordinate programming efforts.

Another goal connected with the exhibit was to involve faculty and students from a wide variety of departments. The panel discussion "To Clone or Not To Clone: Ethical Views from Science and Society" was presented by faculty from biology, English, sociology, and philosophy as well as the University Chaplain. Advertising for this event brought in several high school classes and other community members.

In December 2002, librarians began contacting faculty in their liaison departments to invite student projects that could be showcased along with the exhibit in the following semester. Their efforts resulted in the library's "Frankenstein in Focus" session midway through the exhibition period, with posters from a genetics class (including several on frankenfood) and robots from engineering and computer science students. Electrical "toys" (a Van de Graaff generator, Jacob's Ladder, and plasma balls), originally provided by the physics department for the opening reception, were reactivated by physics students, and "morphing into a monster" makeup was demonstrated by a speech and drama student. Up to 60 students presented at this event; some were simply volunteers, while the students showing their genetics posters were completing a class assignment. As one faculty member commented in an evaluation of the Frankenfest, "The exhibit was great, but even more impressive were the activities on the Trinity side. I thought that the Genetics posters and demonstrations on electricity from Physics added a tremendous amount (and did Trinity proud)."

THE FUN STUFF

When you have a good theme, play it to the hilt! In addition to the educational aspects of hosting the exhibit, staff certainly agreed with Walters' sentiment that a "less altruistic motive was to have a bit of fun and up the library's gate count" (Walters 2001, 9). Most of the advertising was sprinkled with humor, particularly for the less serious programs. The opening reception and costume party set the standard for entertainment and provided some lively moments.

"Ghoulish" food and drinks were served: a head decorated with vegetable munchies (see Figure 5), neon green cookies, fingers in slime sauce (chicken strips with a putrid-green ranch dip), and a "floating arm-of-death" in the swamp water punch (see Figure 6). Body parts from the biology department decorated the food area; a jar with a human brain was stationed at the circulation desk. Trinity's President was made up as Frankenstein's Creature by two speech and drama students, and he gave a short speech before awarding prizes for the best costumes. The electrical toys from physics were demonstrated all evening and remained on display in the library for the duration of the exhibit.

More than 200 people wandered through the exhibit on opening night and enjoyed the party. Visitors received free eyeball key chains, scar tattoos, and glow sticks. Pictures posted on the library web site caught the attention of ALA's Public Programs Office staff, who submitted one for publication in *American Libraries* (April 2003, 9).

The film festival was another fun event in which nine different Frankenstein films were shown during one weekend (see Figure 7). The most unusual was *Frankenweenie*, a black-and-white spoof whose main character, a much-loved dog, was brought back to life by the electrical experimentation of his young owner. This title was highlighted in the film festival advertising in the student newspaper. Even staff members who were not Frankenstein filmophiles rated the movie a thumbs-up. The student film society ran the movies and helped with the advertising. Unfortunately, attendance was very light. Apparently, a beautiful spring weekend in South Texas lured people outside.

WHO PAYS FOR THIS?

Without a budget, advertising and planning programs can be a real challenge. ALA supplied the exhibition and its transportation, with a

FIGURE 5. "Vegetable Head" and Various Body Parts at Opening Reception

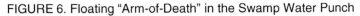

FIGURE 6. Floating "Arm-of-Death" in the Swamp Water Punch

grant from the National Endowment for the Humanities. The rest was up to the library and the university.

An early appeal to ten departments and Trinity's Lecturers and Visiting Scholar's Committee netted $1,150 to support Dr. Lederer's visit. A grant to one of the First Year Seminar faculty covered Dr. Marshall's

FIGURE 7. Ad for Film Festival in Student Newspaper

expenses. The contribution of time and materials from the graphic artist reduced the price for posters, flyers, and table tents by more than $1,000. The University Chaplain not only took part in the cloning panel, but also paid for the refreshments for the informal reception that followed. The Office of Conferences and Special Programs provided generous funding for the opening reception, supplying the final piece of the financial puzzle. In the end, the library spent $1,500 for the Frankenfest, but we all felt that the library's increased campus visibility and positive feedback justified the cost.

WHAT WORKED, AND WHY?

The opening reception, the cloning discussion, and the students' "Frankenstein in Focus" work proved the most successful events in terms of attendance. The reception, held in the library in the evening, attracted at least 200 people, perhaps because it was their first chance to see the exhibit. The free food and party atmosphere enticed some students, particularly those who were coming to the library to study. Publicity, including flyers to all dormitory rooms, posters all over campus, table tents in the dining hall, student center, and library coffee shop, e-mail messages to all faculty and staff, word of mouth promotion by many of the library staff, and major coverage on the University and library web pages, made it difficult to ignore the event, even if one decided not to attend.

The topic for the panel discussion on cloning proved very timely, following by a month the Raylians' announcement that they had successfully cloned a baby. Advertising to high school English and biology classes brought in more people from the community. Students from the First Year Seminar as well as a genetics class were strongly urged to attend by their professors. On a campus where it's a victory to have more than three dozen people attend a lecture outside of classes, we were pleased to welcome over 150.

Many of the evaluative comments from the First Year Seminar students reflected their interest in the Frankenstein in Focus events more than the exhibit itself. As one noted, "I liked the posters that were contributed by the genetics class. I learned a lot from these and it was nice to have students involved in the exhibit, explaining their poster topics." Another student commented, "I liked the exhibits with the electrical phenomena [from the physics department] that you could play with."

Taking on the tremendous job of promoting a visiting exhibition required strong support from the library staff as a whole, as well as major efforts by the "Frankenstein Five" planning committee. A core group of creative and enthusiastic librarians who could take outrageous ideas and make them work proved essential to the exhibit's success, as did the efforts of an energetic library director. Appeals and advertising based on the belief that people would want to participate and/or help contributed to the successes.

Involving the faculty in programs also served to benefit the exhibit. They had much to offer in terms of their expertise, and students gained new insights from their ideas. Furthermore, by participating in these programs the faculty felt more vested in the success of the exhibit and in future activities planned by the library.

In retrospect, it seems ill-advised for a small campus to put on a major exhibition unless it has strong ties to the curriculum. Without the natural connection to the First Year Seminar, it would have been much more difficult to enlist faculty support and to get financial help. In terms of the publicity, it certainly helped to have a theme that caught people's attention.

WHAT DIDN'T WORK?

Programs could have been better attended, but students and faculty lead busy lives and have to make choices based on their own time and priorities. The biggest disappointment was the film festival, which was somewhat expensive (renting the movies or paying for the right to show them in a public forum). The films seemed like a great idea, but the poor attendance may have resulted from a lack of understanding about today's college students and their tastes in film. Doing a quick survey of the library's student workers during the planning stages might have affected the decision to proceed with the film festival.

A FRANK EVALUATION

A successful marketing campaign demands organization, energy, creativity, cooperation, time (*lots* of it), and the courage to try different, perhaps even outrageous, approaches. Meeting the challenges that the Frankenstein exhibit presented to Coates Library required all of those qualities and gave life to skills the organizers had not recognized in themselves. Our success with both the educational and entertaining aspects of the exhibit was reflected in this student comment: "I learned about the history of *Frankenstein*, and I liked the [neon green] footsteps on the floor–nice touch!" Numerically speaking, library usage (the door count) increased over 1,500 during the Frankenfest as compared with the previous February. A number of other major factors have contributed to increased use of the building since 2001 (including the introduction of a coffee shop and the renovation of the main floor to add an information commons), so that by fiscal year 2003-2004 the door count had increased to almost 425,000–a gain of 62% over 2000-01 levels. Coates Library has regained its campus centrality, and some part of that can be directly attributed to the monstrous influence of the Frankenfest and our willingness to experiment with attention-grabbing activities. Trinity's successes and failures with this event may be applied to marketing other kinds of academic library programming and can certainly be added to the body of knowledge about promoting libraries.

QUICK BIB

Bjorncrantz, Leslie, Jeffrey Garrett, and Harrie Hughes. 2000. Northwestern's Art of the Story: Public Relations on a Grand Scale. *American Libraries* 31(11): 50-53.

Frankenstein Site Support Notebook. 2002. Chicago: American Library Association.

Mitchell, Eleanor and Diane Zwemer. 1999. Outside the Exhibit Case: An Undergraduate Library Welcomes the Community. *The Reference Librarian* 67/68: 187-201.

REFERENCES

American Libraries. 2003. 34(4): 9.

American Library Association. Public Programs Office. 2005. *Frankenstein: Penetrating the Secrets of Nature Promotion Guide.* http://www.ala.org/ala/ppo/currentprograms/frankenstein/promotionguide.htm.

American Library Association. Public Programs Office. 2005. *Resources for Public Programming.* http://www.ala.org/ala/ppo/progresources/programmingresources.htm.

Bjorncrantz, Leslie, Jeffrey Garrett, and Harrie Hughes. 2000. Northwestern's Art of the Story: Public Relations on a Grand Scale. *American Libraries* 31(11): 50-53.

Dutka, Andrew, Sherman Hayes, and Jerry Parnell. 2002. The Surprise Part of a Librarian's Life; Exhibition Design and Preparation Course. *C&RL News* 63(1): 19-22.

Frankenstein Site Support Notebook. 2002. Chicago: American Library Association.

Mitchell, Eleanor and Diane Zwemer. 1999. Outside the Exhibit Case: An Undergraduate Library Welcomes the Community. *The Reference Librarian* 67/68: 187-201.

National Library of Medicine. *Frankenstein: Penetrating the Secrets of Nature.* 2002. http://www.nlm.nih.gov/hmd/frankenstein/frankhome.html.

Walters, Peggy. 2001. Collaboration Brings ALA Exhibition to Southern Arkansas University. *Arkansas Libraries* 58(4): 9-10.

Affordable, Effective, and Realistic Marketing

Jane M. Verostek

SUMMARY. Marketing ideas and techniques can be found from observing and surveying patrons in your library. The marketing techniques discussed in this article were utilized over a seven-year period at the F. Franklin Moon Library, a small specialized academic library. These affordable, effective, and realistic marketing techniques include a variety of adaptable ideas including surveys, pencils, screen savers, signage, college newspaper columns, and e-mail. *[Article copies available for a fee from The Haworth Document Delivery Service: 1-800-HAWORTH. E-mail address: <docdelivery@haworthpress.com> Website: <http://www.HaworthPress.com> © 2005 by The Haworth Press, Inc. All rights reserved.]*

KEYWORDS. Academic library, affordable, collaboration, marketing, opportunities, surveys, strategies, techniques, LibQUAL+

INTRODUCTION

This article describes affordable, effective, and realistic marketing strategies that can easily be incorporated into a variety of library set-

Jane M. Verostek (MLS, Syracuse University) is Senior Assistant Librarian and Faculty Member, F. Franklin Moon Library, SUNY College of Environmental Science & Forestry, 1 Forestry Drive, Syracuse, NY 13210 (address e-mail to: jmveros@ esf.edu).

[Haworth co-indexing entry note]: "Affordable, Effective, and Realistic Marketing." Verostek, Jane M. Co-published simultaneously in *College & Undergraduate Libraries* (The Haworth Information Press, an imprint of The Haworth Press, Inc.) Vol. 12, No. 1/2, 2005, pp. 119-138; and: *Real-Life Marketing and Promotion Strategies in College Libraries: Connecting with Campus and Community* (ed: Barbara Whitney Petruzzelli) The Haworth Information Press, an imprint of The Haworth Press, Inc., 2005, pp. 119-138. Single or multiple copies of this article are available for a fee from The Haworth Document Delivery Service [1-800-HAWORTH, 9:00 a.m. - 5:00 p.m. (EST). E-mail address: docdelivery@haworthpress.com].

doi:10.1300/J106v12n01_09

tings. They are based on experiences at the F. Franklin Moon Library, a small specialized academic library located at the State University of New York College of Environmental Science & Forestry (SUNY ESF).

LIBRARY AND CAMPUS OVERVIEW

SUNY ESF is located in upstate New York, adjacent to the Syracuse University campus. Annual enrollment includes 1,700 students (1,000 undergraduates and 600 graduates). Full time faculty totals 141 in fields related to the environment, forestry, and natural resources.

Moon Library staff is comprised of four full-time librarians, one part-time librarian, and six clerical staff. Occasionally, Masters of Library Science students from Syracuse University work at Moon Library in fulfillment of an internship requirement. The Moon Library collection consists of 120,000 physical volumes, however, the library shares a catalog and physical resources with Syracuse University. Currently, the shared library catalog contains 2 million records. Moon Library maintains 1,000 journal subscriptions and shares access to 300+ online research databases.

SURVEYING AS A FORM OF MARKETING

Need to Survey

Moon Library, like many libraries, always seeks to improve our appearance and services. However, staff perceptions do not always match up with patrons' actual needs and wants. To best determine the needs and wants of our patrons, the library conducted two surveys. We developed and administered our own print survey in the spring of 2002. The following year, we participated in the web-based LibQUAL+™ survey, a standardized library service quality assessment instrument. Through our involvement in both surveys, I discovered that the act of surveying can be a very effective form of marketing.

Prior to embarking on a survey, it is crucial to determine whether library staff has the time to devote to such a project, including before, during, and after actual survey administration. Depending on the type of survey and your goals, the types of activities undertaken may include developing survey questions, creating the survey instruments, identifying an appropriate population sample, publicizing the survey to encourage participation, compiling and analyzing results, and possibly following up with respondents. Most importantly, libraries must be prepared to implement changes based on survey results.

When conducting surveys, libraries can intertwine inventive library advertising and marketing efforts into the survey administration process. Afterwards, libraries can advertise and market those library services and resources that have been identified as needing promotion and marketing.

SPRING 2002 CUSTOM SURVEY

During the spring of 2002, Moon Library assessed student and faculty attitudes towards the library through the use of customized surveys, distributed via paper and e-mail. There were several goals for these surveys: to assist library staff in determining how well the library was serving students and faculty; what improvements should be made in terms of library space, services and resources; and where marketing efforts should be focused. In addition, Moon Library also hoped to use survey results to help the library meet the assessment requirements of the Middle States Association of Colleges and Schools accrediting agency. Results would also be used in written library reports that would be incorporated into SUNY ESF's strategic planning initiative.

Survey Content

Brainstorming of survey questions and survey formatting were carried out in library staff meetings. We recognized that the library has two very different patron types (students and faculty) and believed each should have their own specific survey. Using input from all of the library staff, two versions of a print survey were designed in-house, using existing library resources. One librarian did the hands-on work of producing the surveys and subsequently creating survey marketing items (table tents and screen savers) using Microsoft Word, PowerPoint, and Image Carousel software. Drafts of surveys were reviewed by the full library staff until everyone felt both surveys reflected questions we needed answered for both individual departments and for the library as a whole.

The student library survey was produced as a one-page, double-sided booklet titled *A Library Report Card*. Survey questions were separated into three categories: About Library Services, About Library Resources, and About our Facility. The survey was distributed and available to students in highly visible areas of the library over a two-week period.

The majority of survey questions offered respondents a choice of answers. (See Figure 1.) In some cases, we gave respondents an opportunity to explain their choices. This descriptive information gives important insight into why a question was answered as it was. (See Figure 2.) In the final section of the survey, two open-ended questions allowed respondents to share more detailed opinions about the library. (See Figure 3.)

The *Library Report Card for Faculty* was sent to all faculty members as an e-mail attachment several times over a two-week period. Survey questions were grouped into two categories: Library Services and Library Resources. Faculty survey questions were similar to those on the student survey and also included those library services and resources

FIGURE 1. Student Survey: Answer Choice Provided

A Library Report Card: Please tell us how well we are doing. Thank you!

Why do you generally come to the Moon Library? (check all that apply)
_____ to study
_____ to use reserve material
_____ to socialize
_____ to do research (SUMMIT local catalog, databases, etc.)
_____ to attend a meeting
_____ to check email
_____ to search the Internet
_____ to use the writing center
_____ to use the computer lab
_____ to use the services of IDES
_____ to visit the Forest Service office
_____ other, specify: _____

Part A: About Library Services (which do not include the writing center, computer lab, or IDES)

1. How often do you use the Moon Library?
   _____ daily
   _____ weekly
   _____ occasionally

2. Do you ever ask for any library assistance? _____ Yes _____ No

3. Who generally helps you?
   _____ student workers
   _____ a library assistant
   _____ a librarian
   _____ I don't know

4. Are your library needs generally met? _____ Yes _____ No

5. The Library Staff is generally (check all that apply):
   _____ available
   _____ helpful
   _____ pleasant
   _____ other (please specify: _____)

FIGURE 2. Student Survey: Opportunity for Explanations

Do the library hours match your needs? _____ Yes _____ No

Explain: _____

Do the reference desk hours match your library needs? _____ Yes _____ No

Explain: _____

Have you used the reserve collection? _____ Yes _____ No

If yes, have you been satisfied with reserve service? _____ Yes _____ No

Explain: _____

FIGURE 3. Student Survey: Open-Ended Questions

Are there other services you would like to find at Moon Library? _____

Any other suggestions or comments you would like to make? _____

available only to faculty. (See Appendix for the complete faculty survey.)

Promoting the Surveys

To publicize the student survey, informative table tents were placed on tables, at the circulation desk, at the reference desk, and other high-visibility locations in the library. In addition, the screen saver on all public computers in the library included a slide that advertised the survey. For the faculty survey, subjects were contacted solely via e-mail.

Survey Timeframe

Student surveys were distributed at various service points and other locations throughout the library for two weeks during the early part of the semester. Completed surveys were deposited in a designated box at the circulation desk.

Faculty surveys were distributed to faculty via e-mail over a two-week period. Responses were returned to the library director via e-mail.

Survey Responses

Overall, 290 completed student and faculty surveys were returned. Responses were received from 185 undergraduate students (for an 11% response rate), thirty-seven graduate students (6%), and sixty-five faculty (46%).

Students and faculty who provided a name and e-mail address on completed surveys were contacted directly and given personal responses to their questions and concerns. The library director and librarians shared responsibility for making these personal responses. More than fifty individuals were contacted. Survey comments that were received regarding the computer cluster located in the library and maintained by the campus computing department were summarized and sent on to computing staff.

Survey Results

Student and faculty results were summarized and distributed in different formats. Student survey results were compiled into a four-page report which was made available in highly visible areas in the library, published in the student newspaper, and posted on the library web page. The three-page summary of faculty survey results was distributed via e-mail and also posted on the library web page.

Specific student survey items that were identified as needing to be addressed included:

- Assistance with SUMMIT (the library catalog and electronic index and abstract databases) via workshops and informational handouts.
- Larger collection of fiction books and leisure periodicals.
- Access to a lounge area within the library building that provides and allows food and drinks.
- Adequate quiet and group study space.

- Install a change machine in the library building.
- Longer library hours.
- Reference services on weekends.
- Comfortable furniture.

Faculty survey items identified as needing attention included:

- Cannot tell the difference between librarians and library assistants.
- Need assistance with copyright law and guidelines.
- Assistance with SUMMIT (the library catalog and electronic index and abstract databases) via workshops and informational handouts.
- Increase number of electronic index and abstract databases and electronic journals.
- Longer library hours.

Overall, both student and faculty survey results were enlightening. We learned about needs we had not anticipated, such as a way to identify library staff and the students' interest in a fiction and leisure collection. For needs we had expected (e.g., a lounge, assistance with the online system), the surveys confirmed our beliefs, strengthened our resolve to implement changes, and renewed our mission to educate the campus community about existing library services and resources.

SPRING 2003 WEB-BASED SURVEY

A year after conducting our custom survey, there were factors that led us to embark on another library assessment, namely the opportunity to participate in a standardized, national electronic survey via LibQUAL+™ and the anticipation of physical changes in Moon Library.

Survey Content

LibQUAL+™ is a web-based survey of library service quality offered and managed by the Association of Research Libraries (ARL). The questionnaire for the survey was developed by ARL and maintained on the web. When a library conducts a LibQUAL+™ survey, library users are directed towards the web-based questionnaire and ARL, in turn, collects survey responses, compiles survey results, and provides survey data in table, chart, and narrative formats.

Usually with LibQUAL+™, a sample of patrons is selected to receive the survey. However, due to SUNY ESF's small and manageable campus size, the library staff determined it was best to send the survey information to the entire campus population. A total of 2,068 e-mails were sent to undergraduates, graduate students, faculty, and staff.

As done for our 2002 custom survey, we marketed LibQUAL+™ using table tents and the public PC screen savers. The LibQUAL+™ logo was used on all marketing items to add an identity to the survey and to keep all of the marketing items consistent. (See Figure 4.)

Survey Timeframe

Moon Library worked closely with the SUNY ESF computing departments to create an e-mail distribution list for the entire campus population. After the list was created, the library director sent out e-mail communications announcing the survey. Based on LibQUAL+™ guidelines, SUNY ESF students and faculty had eighteen days in which to complete the survey. During this period, the director sent out four e-mails encouraging participation.

LibQUAL+™ is completely anonymous. Though we received narrative comments from a number of participants, we were not able to send personal responses back to them as we did in 2002.

Survey Responses

Of the 2,068 possible responses, 290 were received (oddly this is the exact number of responses received from the spring 2002 paper survey). We heard from 149 undergraduate students, and ninety-one graduate students, thirty-seven faculty, six library staff, and seven college staff members. The student body at the time consisted of 1,700 students (1,100 undergraduates and 600 graduates) and the college employed 141 faculty, 12 library staff, and 274 college staff.

More graduate students responded to LibQUAL+™ (ninety-one) than to our 2002 custom survey (thirty-seven). I attribute this increase to the fact that the LibQUAL+™ survey was distributed via e-mail and the custom survey was only available in Moon Library. Many of our graduate students have office space on campus and do much of their library research using our online system remotely, rarely visiting the physical library.

Faculty responses declined from sixty-five in the 2002 survey to thirty-seven in the LibQUAL+™ survey. It is possible that the faculty

FIGURE 4. LibQUAL+™ Logo

were more responsive to the 2002 survey as it had been customized to particular Moon Library services and resources for faculty.

Survey Results

At the end of the survey period, results for Moon Library could be viewed on the LibQUAL+™ web site. The LibQUAL+™ report containing our survey results was made available to the campus community via e-mail and the library web page. The library also received a notebook with survey results given in color-coded tables and charts, etc. The compilations of statistics were extremely helpful. Overall, students, faculty, and staff were satisfied with library services and resources. The individual respondent free-text comments were also very useful. Of the 290 survey participants, 123 took the time to provide written comments, pointing out a desire for the following improvements:

- Assistance with SUMMIT (the library catalog and electronic index and abstract databases) via workshops and informational handouts.
- Increased number of electronic index and abstract databases and electronic journals.

- Access to a lounge area within the library building that provides and allows food and drinks.
- Adequate quiet and group study space.
- Comfortable furniture.

SURVEY CONCLUSIONS

Results from our 2002 custom survey and 2003 LibQUAL+™ survey clarified student and faculty needs and wishes and allowed the library to determine what library services and resources could be improved. Many of the survey comments could be addressed by ensuring that students and faculty were informed and educated about existing library services and resources. The library staff needed to determine the best way to let students and faculty know that many of the items they were requesting were already in place. To accomplish this, the library staff began a strong initiative to improve our marketing efforts. The library staff decided to focus on the following improvements:

- Creation of a student lounge within the library building.
- Creation of improved library classroom/conference room space.
- Improved signage.
- Larger collection of fiction books and leisure periodicals.
- Weekly library column in the SUNY ESF student newspaper, *The Knothole*.
- Library staff nametags and photographs on the library web page.

Student Lounge

During the summer of 2003, the library worked very closely with college administration to update the library's physical space. A recently renovated and vacated library office space was designated to become a student lounge. The administration and the campus physical plant offices arranged for the campus vending machine provider to install vending machines in the new lounge. Since the college administration manages vending machines on the SUNY ESF campus, they supported the installation of these new vending machines in Moon Library.

The student lounge is located in the basement of the library. It consists of three rooms. The main reading room contains tables and chairs, as well as vending machines. Two adjoining rooms are furnished with couches and comfortable chairs. Furniture for the lounge was obtained by re-arranging furniture in the main library areas.

The lounge rooms are used for students to study or hold meetings in. Students have created their own atmosphere in the lounge and it has become a very popular quiet study area. This was a surprise to library staff. Originally, library staff believed that the lounge would become an area for socializing, but over time students have come to use the space for quiet study. Since the creation of the room, students have made improvements on their own including a bulletin board where student club information, events, etc., are posted.

Creation of the student lounge allowed the library to meet several library user needs: more comfortable furniture, access to food and drink, and adequate quiet and group study space. Marketing techniques have been used to inform students of this new space and to inform them of the need to keep food and drink in this room only. Marketing strategies have included: signage, student newspaper articles, information on the public PC screen savers, and one-on-one communication with patrons.

Improved Library Classroom/Conference Room

More changes to the library's physical space were in motion during the summer of 2003. A non-library office/department was slated to move into the library's existing classroom/conference room. It was imperative for the library to find a new location to take its place. This presented an opportunity to respond to patron and faculty requests for improved library space and increased library instruction. The room chosen to be the new classroom/conference room is immediately inside the library entrance. The print index and abstract collection housed there no longer needed its own room. The collection was consolidated and shifted, shelving was removed, and the room was repainted and re-carpeted. The college administration purchased new chairs to be used in the room, along with tables from the former classroom.

The classroom/conference room is used for Moon Library's credit course on information literacy, brown bag library instruction sessions, and guest lectures. It also serves other campus functions: faculty meetings, student group meetings, theses defenses, student presentations, and campus events (committee meetings, training, and workshops). Marketing techniques including signage and the library screen savers have been used to inform the campus community and library patrons of events taking place in the new classroom/conference room.

Signage

Based on responses from our paper 2002 and 2003 surveys, a need for improved signage emerged. When the surveys were conducted, the library had a collection of signage that had been created over many years by different staff with different designs, colors, fonts, etc. Survey results made it clear that our existing signage was not effective. Students and faculty were asking questions and asking for assistance when signage was in place to direct them and facilitate their use of the library's services and resources.

During the summer of 2003, I collaborated with library staff and the SUNY ESF Instructional Technical Services department (ITS) to create new and consistent signage. After determining the text that was needed and how many signs were required, ITS recommended an overall design. This included the use of a consistent layout, color scheme, and font. The ITS department printed the large format color signs. Their charges ranged from $4.00 each for a 20″ × 20″ sign to $5.00 each for a 24″ × 26″ sign. Once printed, the signs were mounted on foam board that the library had in stock. Smaller (8 1/2″ × 11″) color signs were printed free of charge by the SUNY ESF academic computing department office. To display these smaller signs, the library used clear plastic sign holders or laminated the signs. We selected slanted or slightly tilted clear plastic sign holders (8 1/2″ × 11″ and 3 1/2″ × 10″) which created a table tent look. Prices for sign holders were very reasonable and they were a great investment as they preserve signs from damage. Another way to preserve the smaller signs was to laminate them. Most of our smaller signs were laminated using material we had in house for protecting soft cover books.

Overall, the signage project took several weeks and was handled by one librarian. Signs were created using Microsoft PowerPoint software and campus printing services. At a total cost of approximately $75.00 for printing and sign holders, the project was a great investment that not only more effectively promoted existing library services and resources, but also improved the library's appearance.

Larger Collection of Fiction Books and Leisure Periodicals

One of the areas in the library that received new signage was a set of bookshelves near the library exit. These shelves house fiction books and leisure periodicals donated by library staff and SUNY ESF students and faculty. In surveys, patrons had requested that the library provide this type of reading material. Though such items were not in our collection development plan, we did have the existing bookshelves, which had previously held items that had been withdrawn from the library's collection. By adding donated items, and by marketing this service via signage and articles in the student newspaper, students are now aware of this library service. Items on these bookshelves are free for patrons and they, in turn, may donate items to continue the service. Library staff keep this popular collection stocked by finding resources at local public library book sales and from weeding personal collections.

Student Newspaper

Two of the findings from our LibQUAL+™ survey were that students wanted more electronic resources and more library instruction workshops. This made us realize that students might not be aware of what was currently available to them. As a result, the library looked at ways to market existing resources and services specifically to students.

One of the best ways to reach students and the campus community is to publish in the student newspaper. This is a no-cost way to promote your library. SUNY ESF's student newspaper, *The Knothole*, is published weekly during the fall and spring semesters and is read by students, faculty, and staff. During the summer of 2003, I contacted *The Knothole* editor about giving the library a regular column. The editor was very receptive to the idea and even offered to develop a title and logo for the column. (See Figure 5.)

"Check It Out at the Moon" has appeared in every weekly issue of *The Knothole* since the fall of 2003. All library staff are welcome to write for the column. Topics have included searching for books and journals, electronic databases, e-mail, interlibrary loan, Internet search engines, and the F. Franklin Moon Library web page. The new student lounge was advertised in the column, as were our quiet study areas and brown bag research workshops. Ideas for the columns come from library staff and are frequently responses to reference interviews and comments from patrons. Another resource for the column has been the ALA's @ your library®, The Campaign for America's Libraries web site. The library column takes up one full page (8 1/2" × 11") and word count varies depending on the topic being discussed (300-1,000 words). To write one column takes 1-2 hours a week and columns are submitted every week while classes are in session.

FIGURE 5. "Check It Out at the Moon" Newspaper Column Logo

Nametags and Photographs

Responses from the LibQUAL+™ survey let the library staff know that patrons were uncertain about who to approach in the library for assistance. The library decided to literally market ourselves by wearing nametags to make it easier for patrons to identify staff who could help them.

The first nametag style we tried was a clear plastic sleeve hanging from around the neck. Everyone's name and position were printed on a card that slid inside the sleeve. We ultimately were not satisfied with this style as it did not look professional and staff were having problems with the chains holding the nametags getting caught on furniture, etc.

The staff then tried a brass bar nametag imprinted with the appropriate name and position. These nametags have a magnet that holds them onto most clothing. They are attractive and durable and give patrons enough information for them to know who to approach and/or who they are currently working with in the library. Cost for eleven brass bar two-line nametags purchased from Recognition Products was $125.00. To further enhance our visibility, the library staff also had individual digital photographs taken and mounted on the library web page.

The original clear plastic nametag holders turned out to be very appropriate for our student workers. The cost of supplies for 24 of these nametags including chains was about $30.00 from OfficeMax.

EVERYDAY MARKETING TECHNIQUES

Marketing your library is an "exercise" you do every day. It can take the form of conversations during teaching, reference interviews, campus meetings, library workshops, and conferences. Marketing messages can also be sent in the form of real, tangible items such as pencils, signage, and newspaper articles. Marketing ideas come from observing and listening to patrons. The marketing techniques described here have been utilized over a seven-year period at Moon Library.

Pencils

Patrons frequently ask to "borrow" a pen or pencil from the reference desk. For many years, Moon Library provided golf style pencils with no erasers. After reviewing vendors and prices I recommended to the library director that we purchase full-size pencils and use them to promote the library. The recommendation was accepted and we chose yellow and green, our school colors, for the pencils and text. Each was imprinted with "Visit the Moon www.esf.edu/moonlib." Since 1999, our Friends of Moon Library group has purchased the pencils. We order 2,000 pre-sharpened pencils each year at a cost of $345.00.

Pencils are set out at the circulation and reference desks and are also located by the online public access computers. Pencils are distributed to students in our ESF 200 Information Literacy course, to high school students taking college courses at ESF, to attendees of brown bag library research sessions, and at on-campus and off-campus workshops and conferences.

Screen Savers

When working at the reference desk, take a moment to watch patron behavior, make note of repeated questions, listen to your patrons, and make an effort to address patron needs. One observation I made during a reference desk shift was that the public computers switched to a blank black screen as a screen saver. Many patrons asked whether a computer was out of order because it looked like the monitor was turned off, when actually the computer had just become inactive. Working with our on campus administrative computing department, I converted library-centered PowerPoint presentations to screen savers (using Image Carousel software) and loaded them on all our public computers. The initial purpose of the screen savers was to let patrons know a computer was still turned on, but over time, the screen savers have become a great (and affordable) way to promote the library.

The basis of the screen saver is a series of "slides" that inform patrons about library research tools, due dates, library hours, and special library and campus events. Since implementing the screen savers, campus and student groups have expressed interest in publicizing their own events via the screen saver. Their interest lets me know that the screen savers are noticed by library users and are a successful marketing tool. When I am approached by students and even campus departments to have a slide or two appear in the library screen savers, we work together as a team to determine what the slide(s) will look like and the timeframe they need to run. Each experience with working with student and campus departments has been positive.

Use of screen savers doesn't have to be restricted to computer monitors. When the library's classroom/conference room was relocated, I realized that we could install a soon-to-be-surplused campus television monitor outside of the new location. We decided to run a weekly screen saver that is multipurpose. The screen saver describes events taking place in the classroom/conference room, gives locations and information regarding library displays, offers some library history featuring historical photographs, and provides news about new library services such as the student lounge, library hours, due dates, and other important library information.

This project was a success and was completed using strictly surplus materials. Our administrative computing department had an unwanted television monitor as well as a surplus bracket that would support mounting it from the library ceiling. The campus physical plant installed these items and ran cabling to a surplus computer the library had. All that was required was a CPU with enough memory to run the screen saver. Since the summer of 2003, I have created a different screen saver every week. Campus departments and student groups have also found the television monitor to be a desirable publicity outlet. Each experience working with other groups on their publicity needs has been a positive collaboration and a great way to create campus partnerships.

Creation of weekly screen savers takes just moments (on average 15-30 minutes a week). Screen savers are created using in-house software that the library and campus already had (Microsoft PowerPoint and Image Carousel).

E-mail

Moon Library also communicates library-related information to the SUNY ESF campus via e-mail. The campus e-mail network has created specific e-mail groups, making it easy to target the group you want to reach. Topics of recent e-mail announcements have included:

* News on library services (changes in hours, events, etc.).
* Updates and enhancements that occur regarding our library automation system.
* Availability of electronic databases and e-journals.
* Recent acquisitions of journals and their backfiles.
* Search engine and web site information.
* Course reserve information.
* Copyright information.
* Reminders for scheduling library guest lectures in existing courses.

Campus e-mails are sent as needed and not on a regular basis. The library director and librarians all take responsibility for sending out appropriate e-mails.

FINAL THOUGHTS

Library marketing doesn't have to be complicated, time-consuming, or expensive. Start by listening to library users whether through surveys, observation, or conversation and identify improvements that can be made to meet their needs. Then look for simple, low-cost approaches to let your patrons know about the changes you've made. Affordable and realistic marketing techniques can be very effective in raising awareness about the benefits of using library resources and services.

REFERENCES

American Library Association. 2005. American Library Association @ your library The Campaign for America's Libraries. http://www.ala.org/ala/pio/campaign/ campaignamericas.htm.

Association of Research Libraries. 2005. LibQUAL+™ Charting Library Service Quality. http://www.libqual.org.

F. Franklin Moon Library, SUNY College of Environmental Science & Forestry. 2005. SUNY ESF Libraries. http://www.esf.edu/moonlib.

Janway. [n.d.] Janway Company USA, Inc. http://www.janway.com.
New York Three R's Organization (NYTRO). 2003. LibQUAL+™ Information. http://www.ny3rs.org/AboutLibQUAL.html.
Recognition Products. [n.d.] Recognition Products. Badges/Name tags. http://www. badgesrecpro.com/badges.htm.
RI Soft Systems. [n.d.] RI Soft Systems Image Carousel. http://www.risoftsystems. com/store/ic2.asp.

APPENDIX. Faculty Survey Questions

A Library Report Card for Faculty: Please tell us, how well are we doing? Thank you.

Your name and email address (optional but feedback may be provided if you identify yourself):

_____

Part A: Library Services:

1. Why do you generally come to Moon Library? (check all that apply)
    _____ to do research (SUMMIT catalog, databases, Internet, read journals)
    _____ to sign out books or periodicals
    _____ to place materials on reserve for class
    _____ to attend a meeting
    _____ other, please specify:

2. How often do you use Moon Library? _____ daily   _____ weekly _____ occasionally

3. Do you ever ask for library assistance? _____ Yes   _____ No

4. Who generally helps you with library assistance?
    _____ student worker
    _____ library assistant
    _____ librarian
    _____ I don't know

5. Are your library needs generally met? _____ Yes   _____ No

6. The Library Staff is generally (check all that apply):
    _____ available
    _____ helpful/knowledgeable
    _____ pleasant
    _____ other (please specify:
    _____)

7. Do the library hours match your needs? _____ Yes   _____ No

    Explain: _____

8. Have you used the following Moon Library services?

Service	Used this service?	Rate this service? 1 lowest/10 highest	Suggestions regarding the service
ESF 200 (Information Literacy) (i.e., advise students to take this course)	___ yes ___ no	1-2-3-4-5-6-7-8-9-10	
Consultation with a library faculty member about a library assignment	___ yes ___ no	1-2-3-4-5-6-7-8-9-10	
A "guest lecture" in your class by a member of the Library faculty	___ yes ___ no	1-2-3-4-5-6-7-8-9-10	
Information session on databases, Internet searching, etc.	___ yes ___ no	1-2-3-4-5-6-7-8-9-10	
Interlibrary Loan	___ yes ___ no	1-2-3-4-5-6-7-8-9-10	
Ordering books you recommend for library purchase	___ yes ___ no	1-2-3-4-5-6-7-8-9-10	

Continuation of Part A: Library Services:

9. Do you place reading materials on reserve for your classes? ____ Yes ____ No

      Explain: _____

10. Are you satisfied with this reserve service for your classes? ____ Yes ____ No

      Explain: _____

11. Do you put your reserve materials on a web page for your students? ____ Yes ____ No

APPENDIX (continued)

Part B: Library Resources:

1. Have you used the SUMMIT system? _____ Yes_____ No

2. Do you access SUMMIT from your office (home or other location outside the library)? _____ Yes _____ No

3. Which part of SUMMIT have you used?
   _____ local catalog
   _____ databases
   _____ electronic journals
   _____ other, explain: _____

4. Do you like SUMMIT? _____ Yes _____ No
   Explain: _____

5. Please indicate which specific databases you have used:
   _____

6. Does Moon generally meet your needs for book materials?
   _____ Yes _____ No
   Explain: _____

7. Does Moon generally meet your needs for periodicals?
   _____ Yes _____ No
   Explain: _____

8. Have you visited the Moon Library web site? _____ Yes _____ No
   If yes, have you found the web site helpful? _____ Yes _____ No
   Explain: _____

9. What other libraries do you use?

   _____ Bird _____ SciTech _____ Law _____ Upstate Medical Univ.
   _____ other, specify: _____

10. Have you used the resources/services of the Special Collections/ Archives? _____ Yes _____ No
    If yes, were resources/services helpful? _____ Yes _____ No
    Explain: _____

11. Are the other services/resources you would like to find at Moon Library?
    _____

12. Please offer any comments/suggestions: (Attach additional paper if necessary) _____
    _____
    _____
    _____

Collaborating with Students to Develop an Advertising Campaign

Robert B. Mcgeachin

Diana Ramirez

SUMMARY. The Texas A&M University Libraries undertook a collaborative project with the local American Advertising Federation (AAF) undergraduate student chapter to develop a marketing campaign to advertise the availability of 30,000 netLibrary electronic books. The promotional campaign resulted in the creation of approximately 200 new user accounts and 3,800 e-book circulations within the first two weeks. The campaign of screensaver ads and posters that were developed are still in use for ongoing promotion of the netLibrary e-books. The AAF students benefited from having an ad campaign to include in their personal portfolios and the Libraries gained a creative and undergraduate student-focused advertising campaign. *[Article copies available for a fee from The Haworth Document Delivery Service: 1-800-HAWORTH. E-mail address: <docdelivery@haworthpress.com> Website: <http://www.HaworthPress.com> © 2005 by The Haworth Press, Inc. All rights reserved.]*

Robert B. Mcgeachin (MS, PhD, Texas A&M University; MLIS, University of Texas at Austin) is Associate Professor, Coordinator for Agricultural Library Services, Medical Sciences Library, Texas A&M University, 4462 TAMU, College Station, TX 77843-4462 (address e-mail to: r-mcgeachin@tamu.edu).

Diana Ramirez (MLIS, University of Texas at Austin) is Associate Professor, Senior Social Sciences Reference Librarian, Sterling C. Evans Library, Texas A&M University, 5000 TAMU, College Station, TX 77843-5000 (address e-mail to: dianar@tamu.edu).

[Haworth co-indexing entry note]: "Collaborating with Students to Develop an Advertising Campaign." McGeachin, Robert B., and Diana Ramirez. Co-published simultaneously in *College & Undergraduate Libraries* (The Haworth Information Press, an imprint of The Haworth Press, Inc.) Vol. 12, No. 1/2, 2005, pp. 139-152; and: *Real-Life Marketing and Promotion Strategies in College Libraries: Connecting with Campus and Community* (ed: Barbara Whitney Petruzzelli) The Haworth Information Press, an imprint of The Haworth Press, Inc., 2005, pp. 139-152. Single or multiple copies of this article are available for a fee from The Haworth Document Delivery Service [1-800-HAWORTH, 9:00 a.m. - 5:00 p.m. (EST). E-mail address: docdelivery@haworthpress.com].

Available online at http://www.haworthpress.com/web/CUL
doi:10.1300/J106v12n01_10

KEYWORDS. Advertising campaign, marketing, business students, collaboration, electronic books, netLibrary

INTRODUCTION

Texas A&M University (TAMU), located in College Station, Texas, is a major research institution with an enrollment of over 44,000 students. Through its own purchases and as a member of two consortiums, the Amigos Library Services and the Texas State Library and Archives Commission, TAMU Libraries acquired access to a netLibrary collection of approximately 34,000 e-book titles.

Usage statistics showed that the collection was used infrequently during the first few years it was available. Usage was measured by the number of netLibrary accounts created, the number of e-book turn-aways (indicating a book in use), and the number of e-book accesses. Only about half the netLibrary e-books were initially represented in the online catalog. Access to the remainder of the collection was via a link to netLibrary that was buried under the top-level page of the TAMU Libraries' web site. Even after access was improved by obtaining cataloging for all of the e-books and giving netLibrary more prominence on the web site, TAMU librarians still felt the collection was under-utilized.

TAMU subject specialist librarians have liaison appointments and do outreach to their subject departments on campus. Librarians interact frequently with faculty and students in their liaison departments, developing strong relationships. The close connections between the TAMU business subject specialist and the Marketing Department presented an opportunity to use student marketing expertise to help promote netLibrary.

REVIEW OF THE LITERATURE

Most articles in the library literature on marketing or advertising library resources have focused on promoting services *to* college students. Since the late 1990s, only two articles described *collaboration with* or the *use of* students in the development of marketing campaigns. In both articles, the students gained valuable practical experience that had direct application to their majors and to their future careers.

Kelly (1997) describes how the American Library Association (ALA) worked with design students from the University of Illinois/Chicago to create a series of ads promoting an updated image of America's libraries. She describes how the students were asked to address ALA's communication themes of change, lifelong learning, and of the library as a place providing a sense of community and connection for people.

In another example, Furlong and Crawford (1999) describe the need to bring students and faculty of the University of Maine at Farmington back to the library after a lengthy renovation period. They also needed to increase awareness of the library's electronic resources and its new information literacy program. In this example of student involvement, hiring education majors to help design and implement the curriculum for the information literacy program employed a peer-to-peer approach. The marketing problem was tackled by the collaboration of these education students with the campus Writing Center tutors. The tutors were trained to use the library's core electronic and print resources. With their improved research skills, it was hoped that the tutors would be able to pass the same skills on to their clients in the course of assisting with writing assignments.

METHODS

Librarians at the Texas A&M University Libraries observed that library users often requested "new" services that actually already existed. Clearly, many students and faculty were unaware of the broad range of services offered by the Libraries. More proactive marketing of library services was needed. In the spring of 2001, library liaisons to the Mays Business School at Texas A&M attended the annual Marketing Department awards and recognition banquet. They were seated at a table with students who were members of the local undergraduate chapter of the American Advertising Federation (AAF), a professional society that, at A&M, consists primarily of students majoring in marketing or journalism. The notion of having the AAF students assist the Libraries with a marketing campaign was discussed and contact information was exchanged.

By the fall of 2001, one of those students had become President of the local AAF and the group decided that they wanted to become involved in developing and conducting a marketing campaign for the Libraries. At an initial meeting with the AAF students, the Libraries proposed five possible services that could benefit from advertising: (1) an intra-campus book courier service; (2) netLibrary electronic books; (3) the broad scope and increased number of remotely accessible electronic services;

(4) provision of information and instruction to international students; and (5) branding and marketing of library reference services.

The librarians also shared with the AAF a list of user-preferred advertising methods identified from previous focus group feedback. These included: (1) signs at campus bus stops or on campus buses, (2) partnering with faculty to do presentations in their classes, (3) banners in or on the library or student union building, (4) campus information kiosks, (5) voluntary listservs for notices, and (6) screen saver advertisements on computer monitors in the libraries or in computing labs.

The AAF students selected the promotion of netLibrary e-books, as it was a new and interesting concept to them. Over the course of two months during the fall of 2001, they developed a detailed advertising plan and budget, and then submitted the written proposal to the Libraries for consideration. The objectives of their plan were to: (1) introduce e-books to the students and faculty of Texas A&M University; (2) create an understanding of netLibrary e-books, their features, and how to access them; and (3) increase e-book usage, as measured by the total number of netLibrary accounts created, to 25% of registered A&M students.

The AAF advertising plan proposed the use of traditional media, specialty media, and promotional materials. The traditional media would include: campus newspaper ads, radio public service announcements, flyers for campus bulletin boards, posters hung in the Libraries, banners for the Memorial Student Center building, table toppers for campus dining locations, and brochures to distribute on demand in the Libraries. The specialty media would include: web pages about e-books from the Libraries' and the University's "what's new" sites, screen saver ads on public computer workstations in the Libraries, and an "E-Books Push Week" of intensive advertising. Promotional materials would include: free note holders that attach to computer monitors, sticky strips to go on computer monitors, and stress squeeze balls. Proposed costs were $3,058 for traditional media and $12,628 for specialty and promotional media, for a total of $15,682.

At this point, the Libraries formed a working group to review the proposal and start collaborating with the students on implementation of the advertising campaign plans. The working group consisted of the two library faculty members who had initial contact with the AAF students, the Libraries' liaison to netLibrary, and the members of the Libraries' public relations staff as needed. In December of 2001, a meeting was held with the AAF students to negotiate a reduction in the advertising campaign budget by scaling back or eliminating some of the traditional advertising media and promotional items. The greatest savings, $9,228, was achieved by the elimination of six promotional items that included stress balls, cookies, and customized "goody bags." As a compromise, we deliberately chose to retain one "expensive" (note holders) and one "inexpensive" (sticky strips) promotional item. Traditional media cuts included eliminating glossy double-sided brochures and quarter sheet flyers and reducing the number of full sheet flyers from 2,000 to 1,000 for an additional savings of $887. The reduced total of $5,566 was in keeping with the Libraries' promotional budget and was approved by the Associate University Librarian for Advanced Studies and the Dean of Libraries. A memorandum of understanding about this revised budget and limits on spending was given to the AAF students.

In December and January, the AAF students created an overall advertising theme for the campaign. The idea was to contrast the old traditions, which are ingrained and revered among students on this campus, with new, better, and easier ways of doing things. This was illustrated in a series of three posters with an early twentieth century picture from Texas A&M in the top half and a modern equivalent picture in the bottom half. For example, one poster featured a 1930s black and white photograph of an Aggie bus above a recent color photograph of an A&M shuttle bus. The older photo was captioned "There's the old way . . . " and the recent picture was captioned " . . . and there's eBooks." A one-word slogan, "Easier," "Faster," or "Better" was centered at the bottom of the page, which also included a netLibrary logo, and the netLibrary URL. (See Figures 1 to 3.) This campaign was created from a youthful point of view and was geared to appeal to student tastes on our campus. The "Easier, Faster, Better" dual pictures were designed to attract a student's attention immediately. The URL provided the link to the netLibrary collection as well as to information about creating a netLibrary account.

The images used in the posters were Texas A&M University archival photos and permission to use them in the campaign was obtained from the office of University Relations. Initially, the students wanted to change the color of the netLibrary e-book logo from its trademarked shade of red to maroon. Texas A&M's colors are maroon and white and Aggies are often said to "bleed maroon." Permission was sought from netLibrary to change their logo color for this campaign, but the request was denied and the students used the standard red logo instead.

Once everyone agreed on the campaign theme, identified the media to be employed, and delineated activities for the E-Books Push Week, a

FIGURE 1. "Easier" netLibrary Poster

time line was established. The group designated a lead person for each advertising media component to ensure that deadlines were met. The working group and the AAF students began meeting on a bi-weekly basis in February of 2002 to devise plans and implement the E-Books Push Week by the third week of April 2002.

FIGURE 2. "Faster" netLibrary Poster

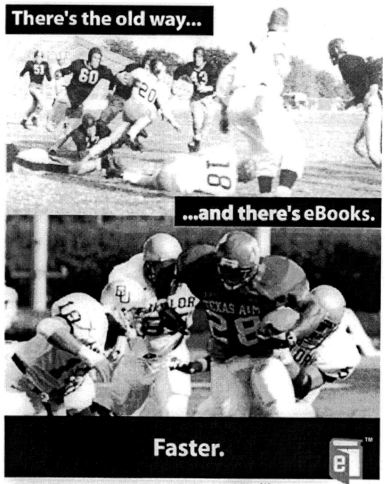

The following activities occurred in preparation for the campaign:

- Web pages explaining how to access, register for, and use netLibrary e-books were created for the Libraries' web site.
- 5,000 sticky strips with the netLibrary URL and the "Easier, Faster, Better" slogan were created for distribution.

- 1,000 Cyber clip note holders with the netLibrary URL and the "Easier, Faster, Better" slogan were created for distribution.
- 750 8 1/2″ × 11″ flyers were created.
- 1,000 8 1/2″ × 11″ and 40 11″ × 17″ color posters were created.
- 500 three-sided table toppers were created. (See Figure 4.) (Campus food services requires that their tag line be added to all table toppers used in their facilities.)
- A link to a press notice about E-Books Push Week was placed on the Libraries' home page.
- A press notice about E-Books Push Week was sent to the campus newspaper, *The Battalion.*
- Computer screen saver versions of the three "Easier, Faster, Better" posters were created.

The E-Books Push Week campaign featured a wide variety of activities. The AAF students did the majority of the distribution and placement work listed below. All occurred in the course of an eight-day period in mid-April of 2002.

- An e-mail message was sent to all 44,000 students promoting the 30,000+ netLibrary e-books. The message contained links to relevant library web pages.
- Two thirty-foot banners were hung over the main hallway of the Memorial Student Center (MSC) and in the Commons of a major campus dormitory.
- An e-books information table staffed with AAF students was stationed under the banners in the main hallway of the MSC one day mid-week to answer questions and distribute flyers, sticky strips, and Cyber clip note holder promotional materials.
- The 8 1/2″ × 11″ flyers were distributed at the table in the MSC and at library service desks.
- Sticky strips were attached to computer monitors in the libraries.
- 250 press kits containing a letter about e-books, a sticky strip, a Cyber clip note holder and an 8 1/2″ × 11″ color poster were distributed to faculty members in departments with subjects heavily covered by the netLibrary collection to encourage them to promote e-books to their classes.
- Forty "Easier, Faster, Better" dual picture 11″ × 17″ color posters were posted in the Libraries.
- An advertisement was run each weekday in the campus newspaper, *The Battalion.* (See Figure 5.)

- 500 three-sided table toppers were placed on tables in campus dining facilities and on study tables in the Libraries.
- 1,000 8 1/2″ × 11″ color posters were placed on campus bulletin boards.

FIGURE 3. "Better" netLibrary Poster

There's the old way...

...and there's eBooks.

Better.

March to a campus computer to log on: www.netlibrary.com

FIGURE 4. Table Toppers for Dining Facilities and Library Study Tables

FIGURE 5. Advertisment in Campus Newspaper

Some components of the netLibrary promotional campaign still appear in the Libraries as ongoing publicity:

- Screen saver versions of the three "Easier, Faster, Better" posters installed on public computer workstations in the Libraries and student computing centers on campus.

- Some of the three "Easier, Faster, Better" posters remain on display in the Libraries.
- There are still some of the sticky strips on computer monitors on campus.

RESULTS

To evaluate the impact of the AAF students' netLibrary advertising campaign, TAMU Librarians analyzed netLibrary usage statistics for the weeks before, during, and after E-Books Push Week. Annual usage trends for the e-books collection were also examined. Reports were generated to analyze the number of netLibrary accounts created by TAMU users, the number of turn-aways (when users could not access an e-book because it was in use or checked out by another patron), and the number of e-book accesses (when e-books were browsed or checked out).

The AAF students' advertising campaign had a moderate effect on the number of new accounts created. (See Table 1.) Our reports showed an average of 4.75 new accounts created per week during the 4 weeks prior to the start of the campaign. The objective was to increase the total number of accounts created to 25% of the student population by the end of E-Books Push Week, but the number of accounts created only reached 3% by the end of 2002. Even though the total number of ac-

TABLE 1. netLibrary Usage Before and After Push Week

netLibrary Usage Before & After Push Week						
	Accounts Created	% Increase*	Turn-Aways	% Increase*	E-book Accesses	% Increase*
Mar 29-Apr 4	5	Na	7	na	377	na
Apr 5-11	5	Na	17	na	512	na
Apr 12-18 Push Week: April 12-19	78	1,642%	57	367%	2,839	634%
Apr 19-25	20	421%	21	135%	1,454	325%
Apr 26-May 3	17	147%	14	−10%	1,094	244%

*Reflects the increase in usage over the average weekly level of netLibrary activity during the four-week period preceding the advertising campaign.

counts created fell far short of the goal, the campaign had a significant impact in terms of percent change in new account registrations at the end of Push Week as compared to the prior weeks. The 25% figure may be a standard marketing goal in the business world, but was perhaps not as realistic in an academic setting. Even though the number of new accounts created actually dropped during the final two weeks of April, the campaign continued to show a positive residual effect as evidenced by the weekly percent change.

The number of e-book turn-aways and accesses followed the same general pattern as that of the new accounts created. While the actual weekly totals did not seem all that impressive, given the relative size of the student population and the number of e-books available, the weekly percent change numbers seem to indicate that the advertising campaign had a definite impact in building awareness of e-books and increasing usage. This impact is most dramatically illustrated by the change in the number of accesses, which increased from a weekly average of 448 accesses to 2,839 accesses during Push Week. Anecdotally, staff members at the Libraries' reference service points reported an increase in the frequency of inquiries related to e-books during the advertising campaign period, with some users asking for assistance in setting up netLibrary accounts.

Looking at the data for the years 2000 through 2004 reveals a significant annual increase in usage of the collection, primarily evidenced by the number of e-book turn-aways and accesses. (See Table 2.) While slightly over 3% of the registered student population had created a netLibrary account by the end of 2002, the year in which the advertising campaign was launched, roughly 11.5% of A&M students had created an account by the end of 2004. Annual totals for e-book turn-aways and accesses show a more dramatic increase over the years following the campaign. The total number of turn-aways and accesses almost doubled from 2001 to 2002 and almost tripled from 2003 to 2004. This indicates a higher demand for access to titles that were being used by other A&M students and a higher demand for access to e-books in general.

The relatively low number of netLibrary accounts created, as compared to the total number of accesses, can be explained in part by the fact that users are not required to create an account in order to view e-books, so some may have chosen not to create an account at the time of the campaign or at all. During the campaign, some users may not have needed to access the features which a netLibrary account offers and could have postponed taking action until a later date. This can partially explain the increase in accounts created in the following years.

TABLE 2. netLibrary Usage for 2000-2004

netLibrary Usage for 2000-2004			
	New Accounts Created	Turn-Aways	E-book Accesses
2000	22	31	978
2001	246	826	13,247
2002	1,071	1,291	23,328
2003	2,678	1,573	36,842
2004	1,922	4,168	62,891

This would seem to indicate that the campaign, including some advertising media still in use today, had more of a long-term impact on usage.

CONCLUSIONS

The advertising campaign created by the AAF students had a positive effect on awareness about e-books and usage of TAMU Libraries' e-book collection. The students' three objectives for their advertising plan were achieved in varying degrees. They were able to introduce e-books to A&M students and faculty with the use of diverse advertising media. They were able to facilitate understanding of e-book features and how to access them through the development of informational and instructional web pages. The students were able to bring about an increase in the number of netLibrary accounts created, though not to the level anticipated in their advertising plan, as mentioned earlier.

The students were able to take a real-world project from an initial concept, through planning and coordination with clients, to implementation, and then finally to seeing the results. They enjoyed working on a campaign that challenged them creatively and produced content that could be added to their portfolios for use in job interviews. The librarians benefited from using student creativity and points of view in the development of an advertising plan that would be aimed primarily at the students' peers. Students created all the graphics in a fairly short period of time and contributed much of the time-consuming work involved in distribution of the posters and other advertising media.

There were only a couple of downsides to this project, but nothing that heavily impacted on the group's ability to work together and produce results. Not all of the students could join the working group for every meeting due to their class schedules, but most were able to attend very regularly. Also, the students were overly enthusiastic about their initial budget proposals. Their experience on this project taught them the differences between realistic advertising budgets in the corporate world versus relatively limited budgets in the library environment.

Libraries should seek more opportunities to collaborate on marketing projects with students who need practical experience. The most likely avenues to pursue would be journalism, advertising, or marketing organizations on campus. Contacting faculty members who might be willing to use a library project as a class assignment would be another excellent option. The undergraduate students involved with the e-books advertising campaign gained valuable hands-on experience that was applicable to their future careers. The librarians benefited from the creativity, enthusiasm, and advertising knowledge that the students brought to the project. Overall, this was a very positive experience for both librarians and students.

ACKNOWLEDGEMENTS

The authors wish to thank Deborah L. Harrington, then a Business Reference Librarian at TAMU Libraries, for her leadership in this project as well as the students of the American Advertising Federation who participated in this project: Jennifer Zajac, Lisa Jankowski, Tiffany McCoy, Diana Suarez, Travis Swenson, and Leigh Richardson. The authors also thank Dr. Fred Heath, then Dean of TAMU Libraries, Charles Gilreath, Executive Associate Dean, and Charlene Clark and Adelle Hedleston of public relations for the TAMU Libraries for their assistance in making this project possible.

REFERENCES

Furlong, Katherine, and Andrew B. Crawford. 1999. Marketing Your Services Through Your Students. *Computers in Libraries* 19(8): 22-5.

Kelly, Joyce. 1997. Generation Xers Create a Campaign for the Library. *American Libraries* 28(2): 60-2.

Implementing an Action Plan: Strategies for Marketing Library Services

Jennifer Campbell
Sally Gibson

SUMMARY. A university library implemented a three-pronged marketing action plan to increase library visibility on campus. The plan included a publicity campaign, a formalized liaison program, and a user satisfaction survey. The year-long effort did return library instruction statistics to earlier levels but did not increase reference usage. Several factors are identified as potential causes for its limited success. *[Article copies available for a fee from The Haworth Document Delivery Service: 1-800-HAWORTH. E-mail address: <docdelivery@haworthpress.com> Website: <http://www.HaworthPress.com> © 2005 by The Haworth Press, Inc. All rights reserved.]*

KEYWORDS. Liaison program, marketing strategies, newsletter, promotion, public relations, READ posters

Jennifer Campbell (BA, Marquette University; MA, Political Science, University of North Carolina, Chapel Hill; MS, Library Science, University of Kentucky) is Government Documents Librarian, Creighton University, 2500 California Plaza, Omaha, NE 68178 (address e-mail to: jennifer.campbell@creighton.edu).

Sally Gibson (BA, University of Kansas; MLS, Texas Woman's University) is Serials & Electronic Resources Librarian, Creighton University, 2500 California Plaza, Omaha, NE 68178 (address e-mail to: sallyg@creighton.edu).

[Haworth co-indexing entry note]: "Implementing an Action Plan: Strategies for Marketing Library Services." Campbell, Jennifer, and Sally Gibson. Co-published simultaneously in *College & Undergraduate Libraries* (The Haworth Information Press, an imprint of The Haworth Press, Inc.) Vol. 12, No. 1/2, 2005, pp. 153-164; and: *Real-Life Marketing and Promotion Strategies in College Libraries: Connecting with Campus and Community* (ed: Barbara Whitney Petruzzelli) The Haworth Information Press, an imprint of The Haworth Press, Inc., 2005, pp. 153-164. Single or multiple copies of this article are available for a fee from The Haworth Document Delivery Service [1-800-HAWORTH, 9:00 a.m. - 5:00 p.m. (EST). E-mail address: docdelivery@haworthpress.com].

Available online at http://www.haworthpress.com/web/CUL
doi:10.1300/J106v12n01_11

As alternative information sources continue to grow, marketing library services and resources becomes increasingly important. Without effective marketing, students, faculty, and staff may fail to recognize the number and quality of library services and resources available (Marshall 2001, 116). Too often, students and faculty do not understand the difference between library resources and those found on the Internet. Several years ago, Ellen Justice, an electronic resource librarian, noted, "[t]he Internet seems to overshadow CD-ROM use because it gets so much coverage and has become so much a part of our culture. Librarians have to actively suggest CD-ROM products as resources" (Jarvis 1998, 74). This same trend continues today with the added complication of distinguishing between library resources such as databases which are delivered through the Internet and the Internet itself. In addition, students and faculty remain unaware of library services, such as library instruction and in-depth reference assistance, that increase their knowledge of library resources and enhance their ability to identify more relevant and higher quality resources for their research.

Academic libraries have been slow to adopt public relations and marketing strategies (Marshall 2001, 116). Administrators, and librarians alike, believe that the library has a captive audience and is a unique supplier of resources and services for professors and students (Marshall 2001, 117). Vicki Ford noted over 20 years ago that academic libraries struggle with the idea of marketing because it implicitly challenges their value in the education process (Ford 1985, 396). Libraries' "role and value in a complex, information-oriented society often is misunderstood or underrated" (Ford 1985, 396). College and university " . . . communities are unaware of their library's resources and fail to challenge its potential" (Ford 1985, 395). In contrast, librarians hold back on marketing because of preconceived ideas about what a library should be (McDonald 2000, 48).

The Reinert/Alumni Memorial Library is one of three libraries on the Creighton University campus, a Jesuit institution located in Omaha, Nebraska, and serves approximately 3,000 undergraduate and graduate students in the colleges of Arts & Sciences and Business.

Falling reference and library instruction statistics, as well as anecdotal evidence, led the staff at Reinert Library to realize that its core audience was unaware of both the resources available in the library and the quality of these resources. In a ten-year period (1990 to 2000), reference statistics fell by thirty-two percent, from 13,009 questions to 8,790 questions. During the same time period, library instruction sessions also fell, from sixty-five sessions in ten subject areas in 1990 to thirty-seven sessions in twelve subject areas in 2000, a decline of forty-three percent. At the same time, reference librarians noted that they were spending more time providing intensive reference sessions (those lasting longer than thirty minutes). This increase was not being captured in the reference statistics because, until 2002, reference questions were divided into two categories: those that lasted less than three minutes and those that lasted longer. In addition, reference librarians reported that during these sessions, students and faculty appeared unaware of the many resources, such as databases, e-books, and online statistical resources, that the library provided. "I looked on the Internet and couldn't find anything" became a common refrain made to librarians during these sessions. Faculty also complained that students were using fewer and poorer quality resources in their papers.

In the spring of 2002, the Reinert Library revised its twenty-year old mission statement to reflect the myriad significant changes affecting library services, resources, and teaching. (See Figure 1.) Two important elements of revising the mission statement were the creation of a set of nine strategic goals for the library and the establishment of assessment methods by which progress toward these goals would be measured. Library staff based these goals on the library's updated mission as well as on external standards developed by the Association of College and Research Libraries.

In fall 2002, the library began to create action plans to address these goals. The action plans detailed steps to be taken as well as specific measures to be used to gauge success. Although assessment has always been a part of library administration, it has become an increasingly important part of demonstrating the library's worth and its importance to

FIGURE 1. Reinert/Alumni Memorial Library Mission Statement

Where We Are Today

The mission of the Reinert/Alumni Library is to provide the services and resources necessary to meet the research and information needs of the Creighton University community. The Library staff augments the educational mission of the University by:

- Developing a collection of diverse and scholarly resources
- Providing the tools and technology that connect people to ideas and information
- Teaching information and research skills

Adopted Fall 2002

the campus community. Two strategic goals were selected for the initial phase of the multi-year plan. These goals were: (1) to anticipate user needs, and (2) to market services and resources.

In January 2003, the library outlined its action plan to anticipate user needs and market services and resources. As part of the action plan, the library worked to increase visibility on campus and in the classroom by enhancing its liaison program, creating a series of National Library Week posters similar to ALA's "READ" poster series, establishing a research assistance program, conducting a student survey, and publishing a new newsletter called "Out of the Blue" news.

LIAISON PROGRAM

First launched in 2001, the faculty liaison program at Reinert/Alumni Memorial Library focuses on creating stronger working relationships between individual faculty and reference librarians.

> Knowing the context in which an academic library operates and conveying what informational resources and services a library can offer to its varied constituencies are keys to the success of a library as a fully integrated part of the academic enterprise. (Wu et al. 1994, 303)

The program provides a structured format for librarians to follow to increase their face time with faculty as individuals or in groups. It also affords librarians an opportunity to make faculty more aware of library services and resources, such as library instruction or the research assistance program.

Dividing the academic departments up based on the interest and academic expertise of the librarians, the library liaison provides all new faculty members in the appropriate discipline with a library orientation, which highlights table of contents alert services, ordering procedures, the instruction program, research and interlibrary loan services, and photocopying privileges. Throughout the year, liaisons send departmental e-mails about new products and services. They send congratulatory messages when a faculty member presents or publishes. Liaisons may also work with departments on accreditation reviews and individual research. The program continues to grow as librarians build relationships with individual faculty members.

A first step in enhancing the liaison program was to make liaison activities more consistent among librarians. The librarians created a list of suggested activities to increase personal contact with faculty. These activities include speaking at departmental meetings, speaking with individual faculty regularly to discover trends or issues, developing course guides that faculty can link to from their class web page or Blackboard courseware, sending an e-mail at the beginning of each semester to promote library instruction and research assistance. A web page describing the program, goals, and activities was added to the library's intranet.

Instruction was also made part of the liaison program. The liaison librarian is responsible for promoting instruction sessions to faculty and for teaching classes in her/his departments. During orientation, new faculty are invited to collaborate on instruction. Since implementing these enhancements, library instruction sessions occur in more departments than before and the total number of sessions returned to 1998/1999 levels. Library instruction continues to be marketed on an individual basis as liaison librarians build rapport with faculty in their assigned departments. While some faculty remain reluctant to use class time for library instruction, most see the advantage of some aspect of classroom collaboration. The liaison program has strengthened the instruction program and, more importantly, broadened its reach across the curriculum. (See Figure 2.)

NATIONAL LIBRARY WEEK "READ" POSTERS

In 2003, the library created a series of "READ" posters (modeled on the successful campaign from the American Library Association) featuring Creighton faculty, staff, and students. Each participant is featured with a favorite book, a word that best describes the participant's attitude towards books, and a paragraph describing the significance of the book selected. Rather than using the word "READ," words like "Evolve," "Think," or "Seek," appear on each poster. (See Figures 3 and 4.) The display, popular with students and faculty, was exhibited during National Library Week in a prominent place at the entrance to the library. A reception was held for all the participants and their colleagues. Notices promoting the exhibit appeared in the online campus newsletter, on the campus cable station, and in flyers distributed across campus. Press releases were provided to local and campus media. As a result of its popularity, the program was repeated in 2004. After National Library Week, the posters hang permanently in the library instruction room.

FIGURE 2. Comparison of BI Sessions and Academic Departments Served

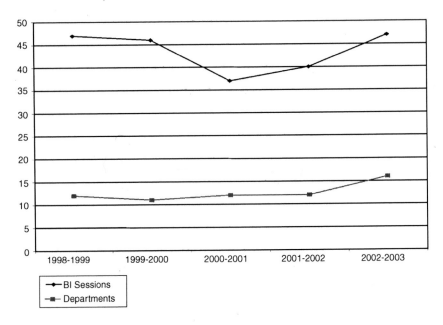

RESEARCH ASSISTANCE PROGRAM

In spring 2004, the library began to heavily promote its research assistance program. This service had been offered informally for several years as an extended reference session at the Reference desk. The Research Assistance Program or "RAP" was created as both a marketing tool and a reference management tool. Students schedule appointments online, describing their topic, assignment, and the sources already consulted. Each session typically lasts forty minutes to an hour and includes instruction on identifying relevant resources. The scheduled appointment gives the librarian opportunity to prepare for the session in advance by gathering resources and preparing sample searches in the OPAC and subject appropriate databases. Early in the spring semester, table tents were placed in the student center and around the library to publicize the RAP program. A campus wide e-mail announced that students could sign up for individual instruction sessions. During the month of the promotion, thirty sessions were held, compared to fourteen

FIGURE 3. "READ" Poster Featuring Premchand Nair, Mathematics/Computer Sciences Department Faculty

sessions in February 2003. The Reinert librarians had believed "RAP" could help more students if they knew about it. And indeed, when the word got out, more students took advantage of the service.

STUDENT SURVEY

In order to learn what users wanted and needed from the library, Reinert Library administered a library satisfaction survey. To avoid the cost and time involved with pre-packaged surveys such as LibQUAL+, the library created and administered its own instrument. A mixed format of thirty multiple-choice and four free-response questions was used. (See Figures 5 and 6.)

FIGURE 4. "READ" Poster Featuring Carol Zuegner, Journalism Department Faculty

Flyers were hung around campus a week before the survey. During the week of the survey, library student workers and staff went to four different locations to distribute them. As an incentive, students who turned in a completed survey got a candy bar. The survey was also posted on the library's home page.

After speaking with the campus assessment office, the library determined it did not need a statistically significant response rate for the survey because it was only interested in discovering general trends of satisfaction or dissatisfaction. The 410 survey responses out of 500 surveys distributed provided a baseline picture of the overall student satisfaction with library staff, resources, and services. The library staff received high satisfaction ratings for service and service quality. Resources also generally received high scores with graduate students

FIGURE 5. Reinert/Alumni Memorial Library 2003 Student Survey

Receive a free candy bar! and help the Reinert/Alumni Library serve you better at the same time. Please darken one bubble per item. Thank you!

	1	2	3	4	5
What is your class standing? (1) = First Year (2) = Sophomore (3) = Junior (4) = Senior (5) = Graduate ---------------------------------->	O	O	O	O	O
What is your College?	O	O	O	O	O
(1) = Arts & Sciences (2) = Business (3) = Univ College	O	O	O	O	O
(4) = Graduate School --------------------------------------->	O	O	O	O	O
What is your gender?	O	O	O	O	O
(1) = Female (2) = Male -------------------------------------->	O	O	O	O	O
Where do you live?	O	O	O	O	O
(1) = On campus (2) = Off campus --------------------------->	O	O	O	O	O
(1) = Daily (2) = Weekly (3) = Monthly **(4) = Twice a Semester (5) = Rarely/Never**					
1. I use the library . . . to study or prepare for class.	O	O	O	O	O
. . . to do research or locate information for class.	O	O	O	O	O
. . . to type and/or print class assignments.	O	O	O	O	O
. . . to socialize or use the computers for recreation.	O	O	O	O	O
	O	O	O	O	O
(1) = Strongly Agree (2) = Agree (3) = Disagree **(4) = Strongly Disagree (5) = NA**	O	O	O	O	O
1. The current library hours meet my needs.	O	O	O	O	O
2. I can find a suitable place to study in the library.	O	O	O	O	O
3. The library building is inviting and functional (furniture, lighting, etc).	O	O	O	O	O
4. I can use the library web site from my residence as needed.	O	O	O	O	O
5. The library has . . . the books that I need.	O	O	O	O	O
6. . . . the magazines and journals that I need.	O	O	O	O	O
7. . . . the full text (electronic) resources that I need.	O	O	O	O	O
8. . . . the videos that I need.	O	O	O	O	O
9. I can find library materials shelved in the proper place.	O	O	O	O	O
10. I can find a computer workstation when I need one.	O	O	O	O	O
11. The computers in the library have the capability that I need.	O	O	O	O	O
12. The library web site is clear and easy to navigate.	O	O	O	O	O
13. The Creighton Libraries' online catalog is clear and easy to use.	O	O	O	O	O
14. The photocopiers are adequate for my needs.	O	O	O	O	O
15. The microfilm and microfiche printers are adequate for my needs.	O	O	O	O	O
16. The Circulation/Reserve staff is responsive to my needs.	O	O	O	O	O
17. The Reference staff is responsive to my needs.	O	O	O	O	O
18. The Periodicals staff is responsive to my needs.	O	O	O	O	O
19. Interlibrary loan service meets my needs.	O	O	O	O	O
20. I feel adequately prepared to use the library for research.	O	O	O	O	O
21. My classes do not require me to use library resources.	O	O	O	O	O
22. I am satisfied with the library's ability to meet my needs.	O	O	O	O	O

Thank you! Please give us your comments on the reverse side of this form.

FIGURE 6. Student Survey Free Response

List any subject areas or information resources that you feel are inadequate in the library's current collection. Please be specific.
Please describe any technological improvements you would like to see in the library, including the web site, computers, software, etc.
Other than the library, where do you look for the information you need? Please be specific.
Other comments or recommendations:

Thank you!

Name _____

E-mail or phone _____

showing a higher dissatisfaction than undergraduates. Respondents also expressed a desire for more computer workstations loaded with a variety of software programs. Individual written comments indicated which resources and services should be improved.

OUT OF THE BLUE NEWS

"Out of the Blue" news is a series of bi-weekly e-mails, a simple and effective way to promote library resources and services. It differs from Creighton University's online daily newsletter in two important ways. "Out of the Blue" contains information about the library alone. Secondly, it is very short, usually one or two succinct paragraphs, making it easier for faculty and staff to identify the information relevant to their needs. The bi-weekly e-mails also provide a mechanism for the library to remain in the public eye and remind the community of our resources and services.

RESULTS–ONE YEAR LATER

Reinert/Alumni Memorial Library focused on marketing as an important strategy to address declining library instruction and reference usage. As part of the action plan, the library worked to increase visibility on campus and in the classroom by enhancing its liaison program, creating a series of National Library Week posters similar to ALA's "READ" poster series, establishing a research assistance program, conducting a student survey, and publishing a new newsletter called "Out of the Blue" news. While there was some success for individual programs, the overall impact was incremental. The library increased its exposure to academic departments, which is evident both in the increase in the number of departments requesting library instruction and in the success of the RAP program. This exposure reversed the trend of declining instruction statistics and provided new methods for capturing reference interactions.

Reinert Library's marketing efforts were disjointed in that the library lacked an overall plan to coordinate the departments' action plans. Departments promoted their individual services, but a library-wide effort was not developed. Without one person to be responsible for its planning and implementation, to initiate and coordinate marketing projects, and to keep the library in the community eye, the library fell short of its strategic goals to anticipate user needs and market library services and resources. The positive response to the liaison program, student survey, and research assistance program, however, highlight the effectiveness of actively marketing library services and resources. Coordination of marketing efforts would channel our energies even more productively.

QUICK BIB

Marshall, Nancy. 2001. Public relations in academic libraries: A descriptive analysis. *The Journal of Academic Librarianship* 27 (Mar.): 116-121.

REFERENCES

Ford, Vicki. 1985. PR: The state of public relations in academic libraries. *College & Research Libraries* 46: 395-401.

Jarvis, Margo. 1998. Anatomy of a marketing campaign. *Computers in Libraries* 18: 74-78.

Marshall, Nancy. 2001. Public relations in academic libraries: A descriptive analysis. *The Journal of Academic Librarianship* 27: 116-121.

Wu, Connie, Michael Bowman, Judy Gardner, Robert Sewell, and Myoung Chung Wilson. 1994. Effective liaison relationships in an academic library. *College and Research Library News* 55: 303.

We Better Get This Party Started!

Lisa Lavoie

Judith Markiewicz

SUMMARY. Each fall, the Tunxis Library hosts a party. Usually thematic, sometimes didactic, and always cerebral, the library uses the party to communicate our "party line" to the entire campus community: *we are here to make your life easier.* It's particularly effective when delivered at the start of the semester, before the unrelenting rhythm of classes, committee work, and meetings has begun.

Showing the campus community that the library is here to support them is our core theme, wrapped in a party context. Our goal is to create a party that jump-starts the fall semester for everyone. In this article, we describe our most recent parties, focusing how we develop, plan, and execute these promotional initiatives, with little money, but plenty of creativity and teamwork. *[Article copies available for a fee from The Haworth Document Delivery Service: 1-800-HAWORTH. E-mail address: <docdelivery@haworthpress.com> Website: <http://www.HaworthPress.com>* © 2005 by The Haworth Press, Inc. All rights reserved.]

Lisa Lavoie (BA, University of Connecticut; MLS, Southern Connecticut State University; EdD in process, University of Hartford) is Librarian, Tunxis Community College Library, 271 Scott Swamp Road, Farmington, CT 06032 (address e-mail to: llavoie@txcc.commnet.edu).

Judith Markiewicz (BA, Eastern Nazarene College; MLS, University of Rhode Island) is Director of Library Services, Tunxis Community College Library, 271 Scott Swamp Road, Farmington, CT 06032 (address e-mail to: jmarkiewicz@txcc. commnet.edu).

[Haworth co-indexing entry note]: "We Better Get This Party Started!" Lavoie, Lisa, and Judith Markiewicz. Co-published simultaneously in *College & Undergraduate Libraries* (The Haworth Information Press, an imprint of The Haworth Press, Inc.) Vol. 12, No. 1/2, 2005, pp. 165-186; and: *Real-Life Marketing and Promotion Strategies in College Libraries: Connecting with Campus and Community* (ed: Barbara Whitney Petruzzelli) The Haworth Information Press, an imprint of The Haworth Press, Inc., 2005, pp. 165-186. Single or multiple copies of this article are available for a fee from The Haworth Document Delivery Service [1-800-HAWORTH, 9:00 a.m. - 5:00 p.m. (EST). E-mail address: docdelivery@haworthpress.com].

KEYWORDS. Parties, library promotion, library marketing, community colleges, teams

INTRODUCTION

Summer is often the time of respite for academic library staff members, a time to clean desks, revise library handouts, and perhaps take that long-awaited vacation. Unless, that is, you are on the staff of the Tunxis Community College library. For us, summer is the beginning of a major creative inoculation . . . it's party time.

Each fall, the Tunxis Library hosts a party. Usually thematic, sometimes didactic, and always cerebral, the library uses the party to communicate our "party line" to the entire campus community: *we are here to make your life easier.* And when that message is couched in food, cleverness, and festivity, they hear it and they remember it. It's particularly effective when delivered at the start of the semester, before the unrelenting rhythm of classes, committee work, and meetings has begun.

With little in the way of discretionary funds for public relations and virtually no budget for marketing, what we lack in funds we must make up for in creativity. Showing the campus community that the library is here to support them is our core theme wrapped in a party context. Our goal is to create a party that jump-starts the fall semester for everyone.

Tunxis Community College is a small, suburban community college in Connecticut, just twelve miles west of Hartford. It serves approximately 4,000 full- and part-time students enrolled in credit courses, sixty-plus full-time faculty, as well as adjunct faculty, staff, administrators, and community patrons. The library currently has one director, three full-time librarians, three part-time librarians, three library associates, and one secretary.

THE PARTIES

It occurred to us several years ago, that though we spent tremendous time and energy relentlessly promoting every new resource and service the library provided, we neglected to celebrate our greatest asset: our patrons. To fill this promotional void, we decided to extend our slogan, "we make your life easier," to include terms like "richer," "happier," and "more collegial." To make our patrons lives richer, happier, more collegial, and often more caffeinated, we began designing library parties for the college. We started this process by inviting just one patron group at a time. Our first parties were created exclusively for the faculty. We then began designing parties for the classified staff. Eventually, we expanded our party invitation list to include the entire campus community (faculty, staff, administration, and students). We have been designing library parties for almost ten years now and one thing is clear: our patrons appreciate the attention and their appreciation has created a strong patron loyalty to the library and a very positive ethos for the college.

Unknowingly, we were intuitively following a well-known business premise: that a client appreciation event, such as a party, can increase client retention, client loyalty, and sales. Businesses, such as CompuSmart in Toronto, utilize the party concept to "get clients into an environment where they can let loose and have a good time . . . a form of currency which pays huge dividends into the relationship" (Seymour 2004).

Corporate entertaining has always been part of the marketing process and even home-based entrepreneurs selling cosmetics, toys, and crystal know that presenting products in an informal yet festive environment yields better sales (Cohen 1987). For us, the parties have not only yielded better "sales" in terms of exposure to our resources and services, but have garnered even better commodities: the respect, appreciation, and admiration of our patrons.

The Faculty Survival Kit

Playing off the popular television show, *Survivor*, we designed Faculty Survival Kits for all of our full-time faculty members. The kits (actually large burlap sacks tied with twine) were labeled with laminated "dog tags" made by stenciling on "wrinkled paper" stationery. Each tag identified the faculty member by name and by library card barcode number. On the outside of the bag we stenciled "FACULTY SURVIVAL KIT," in block letters. Inside, the contents of the sack included bottled water, a large chocolate bar, a list of the librarians' "Top 10 Books for a Desert Island," a description of great information literacy-based assignments, a faux treasure map for finding our newest databases, homemade bookmarks designed with an "information jungle" or "library as oasis" theme, and an antiqued "take-out" menu of the library's online, phone, and personal information services. We heaped the bags in the middle of the lobby of the campus's faculty wing early one morning in the beginning of the fall semester, so faculty members would have to paw through them to find their own personalized survival kit.

The "party" was an individual invitation to each faculty member to come to the library and join us for a free cup of coffee or tea anytime during the semester at his or her convenience. We included this invitation in the form of a tea-stained coupon, assuring them that the trip would be even more stimulating than the beverage. The number of coupons redeemed gave us an accurate accounting of how many faculty members actually visited the library (a little over one-half), and since the object of the free coupon was to get faculty in the door, we felt we had attained our goal.

The success of this promotion was resounding, as faculty members actually shrieked with delight at the personalized and clever approach–many of them joining us for coffee immediately. Not only did we delight faculty members, but we also won the College's "Kudos of the Month" award at an all-campus ceremony recognizing departments or individuals who have provided an extra effort to lift campus morale, provided a special service, or otherwise added a meaningful spark to campus life at Tunxis.

A Library Menu of Rich Possibilities: The Information Literacy Bistro for Faculty

The Information Literacy Bistro grew from the following staff discussion points:

1. We knew we had a professional imperative to build a strong information literacy program for our students and that meant we needed to update the entire faculty on the various courses, tours, and workshops we could create and make available to them to supplement their classes.
2. The college and the library had both included Information Literacy as one of the goals for implementation in the current Strategic Plan.
3. The library had interviewed traditionally aged students (17-24 years) about their perceptions of instruction classes and the results of these interviews yielded some important changes in our own teaching goals.
4. It was time for a party.

With these four points in mind, we decided to create an engaging means of communicating the library's information literacy goals to the faculty. We enlisted the help of our Academic Dean, who gave us carte blanche to design the agenda for the first faculty meeting of the fall semester. This was no small privilege, as the first faculty meeting is considered the most important meeting of the semester. The Dean also agreed to keep our meeting plans secret and scheduled a routine faculty meeting in the largest meeting space on campus.

We transformed the meeting space into a bohemian bistro. We arranged the tables in different angled positions around the room and covered them with differently colored and textured tablecloths. We topped the tables with mason jars filled with wildflowers and pottery pitchers (from our home collections) for ice water and lemons. Each table also had several baskets filled with grapes, cheeses, and specially ordered honey whole-wheat baguettes from a local supermarket. We found clear plastic cups decorated with purple swirls and the world "rage-a-licious" at the dollar store to use with the lemon water on the tables. We also had a variety of colored napkins and paper goods at each place setting. We hung groovy iridescent beads at the entrance doorway and because one of the librarians owned one, we had a life-sized cardboard stand-up of James Dean pointing faculty toward the coffee. James Dean was also holding a handmade sign reading "Drink coffee as if you'll live forever . . . ," loosely based on a famous Dean quotation. ("Dream as if you'll live forever, live as if you'll die tomorrow.") We played Frank Sinatra CDs. We brewed our own coffee and had various teas available as well. We also designed a restaurant-quality menu for each place setting, however, instead of listing food and drinks, ours offered *"The Tunxis Library Menu of Rich Possibilities for Information Literacy."* (See Figure 1.)

We used ivory manuscript stationery for the menu, and created an elegant menu cover in-house using teal, black, and burgundy scripted lettering and formal graphics. Around the fold of the menu, we tied a thin gold cord with a bottom tassel, and we lined the inside of the menu with light blue paper. Appetizers, entrée, and dessert choices inside the menu included "The Library Tour," "The Assignment-Driven Library Instruction Class," "Hot Topics," and other instruction alternatives. (See Figures 2a and 2b.)

Having the support and trust of the Academic Dean was the essential ingredient to the success of the Library Bistro. She gave us the unbeatable forum of the first fall faculty meeting and let us make information literacy the entire agenda. Faculty members came into the meeting and

FIGURE 1. Library Menu of Rich Possibilities

were floored by the transformation of the space. They seemed to really enjoy the restaurant ambiance and they loved the personal attention. The room was abuzz with laughter and talking, and, from the moment of entry, we knew we had hit a right note for the beginning of their semester. We had the attention of approximately sixty-six full-time faculty members and some members of the adjunct faculty–we set up the tables for eighty people and filled the house.

After a bit of socializing, the library director formally introduced our information literacy topic and the librarians took the stage, speaking in turns about the Tunxis Information Literacy Project. We used a short, light-hearted PowerPoint presentation in the spirit of mixing business with pleasure. We also encouraged faculty to read the menu and begin ordering one or more of our instruction options.

The party was certainly one of our most didactic experiences, as we really did need to impart some serious information: based on our survey of students born after 1980, we learned that our students are much less interested in personal anecdotes and in general instruction on how research databases could be searched, and more interested in learning what they need for the assignment, getting online, and getting the assignment completed. We also learned that these students came to the college with the perception that a college library is an overwhelming and frightening place and the perception that librarians were sad, lonely women. We wanted to make our library courses effective for this younger cohort of students and to change those perceptions, and we needed the help of the faculty to make it work–to us, this called for a party.

One would assume that our requests for library instruction would increase dramatically after this party. Regrettably, they did not. However, we did note that faculty who had used our instruction services infrequently in the past renewed their interest in library instruction by bringing in their classes. We saw an increase in faculty interest for our hot topics courses (short, informative sessions) and collaborative faculty/librarian initiatives that covered the entire semester. We also noticed improvements in library-related assignments, with a better focus on raising students' information literacy skills.

Going Bananas at the Library

We honor the college's classified staff each year. The classified staff is comprised of the secretaries, administrative assistants, clerks, typists, and maintenance and security staff who do so much behind the scene. The Classified Staff Association (CSA) meets monthly at various loca-

FIGURE 2a. Information Literacy Menu Offerings

*Please choose any selection or combination
of selections listed on the opposite page.*

*Each selection arrives replete with side
orders of warmth, humor, and the
milk of human kindness.*

Served up by your Tunxis Librarians.

tions around the campus and once a year we ask them to be our guests in the library. The first time we hosted the CSA meeting, we threw a party with the theme, "Going Bananas at the Library." Because we value the exemplary work and personalized service these individuals offer to the college community and the public, we created a party to keep them healthy, based on wellness, exercise, good health, and stress management.

We displayed our collection of videos, books, and audio books on the subjects of yoga, Pilates, weightlifting, stress management, ergonom-

FIGURE 2b. Information Literacy Menu Offerings

Appetizer

The Library Tour   15 Min.
*A whirlwind tour highlighting the myriad services and
resources of the Tunxis Library.*

House Specialty

The Wired Library   45 Min.
*An improvisational Library classroom experience
showcasing online resources and the many services
available to students.*

Healthy Choice

The Assignment-Driven Library Instruction Class   45 Min.
*What we hope will become a perennial favorite for faculty!
Library instruction will be designed in collaboration with
the instructor and focused on how best to complete the
research assignment.*

Catch of the Day

Advanced Subject-Specific Research Class   45 Min. to 1 Hr.
*Librarians collaborate with faculty to design a Library
research class focusing on the higher level resources
available for course-related topics.*

Dessert

Hot Topics   Varies according to market
*The Librarians host a very short informational session on
the hot topic of your choice! Topics include: plagiarism,
citing resources, MLA and APA, finding scholarly journals,
evaluating Internet websites, choosing a great research topic,
or organizing a research paper.*

*Librarians can modify any of the above
selections to accommodate individual tastes.*

ics, workplace health, nutrition, and vitamins, and friendship on the tables used for the meeting. The décor was tropical, with brightly colored tablecloths, grass table skirts, and colorful napkins and paper goods. We played lilting Island music and served fruit salads, cheese and crackers, organic coffee, herbal teas, and juices.

These events are particularly satisfying for us, as classified staff members are very active users and supporters of the library, many of them having begun their careers as students at the college, and many of them with children who also now utilize the library collection on a regular and enthusiastic basis.

The Fabulous Fete

In the spirit of the popular local bookstore/coffee haunts, the Tunxis Library staff opted to turn the library into its own paean to books and coffee: a Library Café Party. Using our own in-house talents, we designed beatnik-inspired invitations for faculty, staff, and members of the administration. We labeled each invitation with the individual's name and delivered them through the campus mail system.

Decorating the library's study tables with red and white checkered tablecloths and candle-dripped wine bottles, the staff created retail-inspired book displays of our newest fiction and nonfiction in various designs and situated them in various locations around the library. French café music permeated the air, as the library staff dressed in black pants, white shirts, and brightly colored bandannas (worn on individually chosen areas of their bodies) and waited on and mingled with faculty, staff, administrators, and students with hand-carried plates of cheese, crackers, coffee, and home-baked goods (showcasing the staff's culinary talents was a true cost-saving measure). Guests were encouraged to browse, sit, linger, chat, and eat with each other. We had designed seating for 100-plus guests and allowed plenty of standing room. There was not an empty seat in the house during the two-hour event.

Putting on the Glitz: Celebrating the Tunxis Authors

Partnering with the college's Student Activities Department, the library hosted a "black tie" party, inviting the entire campus community (students, too) to don formal festive attire and socialize with the faculty and staff of Tunxis who had authored and published a written work.

The invitations for this event were designed in-house with a black and white tuxedo motif (we affixed gold stars on the front for pizzazz) and were sent individually to faculty, staff, and members of the administration. Invitations enlarged to poster size were displayed about the campus to invite students to the event. We decorated the library with black and gold balloons and used gold wrapping paper from the dollar store on all the library tables. Having the Student Activities Department assist with the food, funding, decorating, and publicity helped tremendously.

Our interest in co-hosting the party with the Student Activities Department was based in part on previous positive collaborations, as well as our gratitude for being the recipient of several generous student class gifts. We saw the Fabulous Fete as an opportunity to continue this strong working relationship and provide a social and literary event wherein students could meet and mingle with faculty, staff, directors, deans, and the college president.

The authors' published pieces, displayed with corresponding description placards, were available for guests to peruse. We selected authors to read from their books of poetry, dissertations, novels, textbooks, articles, and editorials, focusing primarily on new faculty and staff in an effort to introduce them to their colleagues and the students. Guests were treated to refreshments including coffee, tea, punch, and strawberries dipped in chocolate, and a piano was moved into the library for musical interludes between readings. The pianist was a student who graciously shared her talents for the event. Over 300 people attended this event during the course of two and a half hours. The beauty of this party was in celebrating the successes of our co-workers at a festive and formal affair in the middle of a workday afternoon.

You Belong Here

Looking at Abraham Maslow's famous hierarchy of human needs, we saw a definite correlation between a trip to the Tunxis Library and a trip up the Maslowian pyramid to self-actualization–leading us to design the "You Belong Here" party for the campus. In keeping with the hierarchy, the party started off with lots of food and drink, provided safety and comfort, ensured friendship and belonging, instilled social acceptance and self-esteem, celebrated art, literature, and the environment, shared our love, and left room for all kinds of self-actualization.

Each member of the faculty, staff, and administration received a personalized, hand-delivered invitation, this time in the form of a white paper bag labeled "You Belong Here." We were careful to include everyone on the campus; including the full- and part-time staff members of the cafeteria, bookstore, and maintenance departments (these employees are often forgotten because of their late night or early morning work schedules). This comprehensiveness required some diligent research of the various employee staff lists. Students were invited to the party via large posters (invitations enlarged to poster size), which we located on easels in the college's lobbies and at the entrance to the library.

The invitation was inspired by the pyramid shape of Maslow's Hierarchy and attached to a small white prescription bag. Inside the bag, we included small white candles, white promotional bookmarks, white stress balls (which were imprinted with our slogan: "We Make Your Life Easier" and our web site address), white pens, white candies, and white fortune cookies (coconut-flavored cookies baked with different famous library quotations as the fortunes). We decided to utilize a white theme for every aspect of the party, as we began to see ourselves as clinicians prescribing just the right tonic for the beginning of a new semester.

The library staff wore white lab coats (borrowed from the Chemistry Department), in keeping with our clinical theme. We served white food, including a large white cake that read, *"At the Tunxis Library You CAN Have Your Cake and Eat It Too!,"* as well as white cookies, white cupcakes, white brownies, white popcorn, and white donut holes. We decorated the library in white as well, with white tablecloths, white balloons, white napkins, white cups, and white plastic ware. White chocolate and French vanilla coffee was served, as well as the infamous "white soda" which we served from a rented champagne fountain.

We never tracked the attendance for this party, though based on our collective level of fatigue from talking, we knew we had succeeded in capturing the attention of our invitees. We quickly learned from this party to add an ending time to subsequent party invitations, thus dodging the potential of having the inevitable stragglers show up just when food and energy levels are near depletion.

(A more detailed article on this party can be found in the journal, *MLS: Marketing Library Services*, July/August 2002, pages 1-3.)

We Know We Look Different

Perhaps our most absurd party theme, the "We Know We Look Different" party was created on the summer day we decided to re-arrange all the furniture and computers in the library for a new look. Coinciding with this furniture rearrangement was a redesign of the library web page and the addition of new electronic databases to the collection. This set of changes inspired us to ask one of the college's graphic designers to take a studio photograph of the library staff wearing costumes of our own design. (See Figure 3.) The library director became a gypsy fortuneteller, reference librarians dressed as a construction worker, a loony chef, and a mad scientist, the library associates were farm girls and fan dancers, and the secretary was a lounge singer. We used this photograph

FIGURE 3. We Know We Look Different

on the cover of a personalized invitation, luring the faculty, staff, and administrators to find out just how different we looked. Inviting everyone to "eat, drink, and be merry in the information arcade," we promised to ply them with all the ways we would make their lives and the lives of the students better.

We served coffee (in coffee pots brought in from home) and homemade pastries and cupcakes for the event and through informal conversations we were able to show and talk about the new website and electronic databases. The response to this event was terrific, as the college community had never seen the usually staid staff of the library look this bizarre before, and the curiosity factor led to a very crowded library.

Magical Realism: Mingling the Marvelous and the Real

We believe that magic is created every day at our community college. A magical realism party seemed the perfect way to celebrate the mingling of the marvelous and the real. This party was easily our most ambitious. Magical realism is both a literary and artistic term used to describe works that portray unbelievable and impossible things routinely happening in the midst of perfectly ordinary events. Since we strive to use an intellectual theme as the basis for our parties, we were able to tell the campus community how marvelous they really are, showcase the many books and films we own of this genre, *and* create a fantastical and colorful décor for the library.

Among our challenges was to convey magical realism without looking like a makeshift Harry Potter set or having to over-explain the concept. To overcome this challenge, the term "magical realism" had to be defined in the invitation. We designed personalized invitations in the form of small iridescent organza pouches (purple, gold, turquoise, and pink) with matching silk tassel ties. In each pouch we added a gold coin (chocolate), a couple of brightly colored feathers, and a very small color-printed invitation that read, "*Magical Realism is an art of surprises–the mingling of the marvelous and the real. Celebrate the magical realism of the Tunxis Library and we'll mingle with you, marvelous you.*"

We also added another small piece of paper to the pouch with each staff member's name and the following directive: "*Sometimes a book finds you. This call number matches a book in the Tunxis Library. You've been brought together. Why?*" At the bottom of this piece of paper we added the call number of one of the more esoteric, but interesting titles in our collection. Each staff member was randomly matched with a title and we hoped each person would be curious enough to come into the library, find his or her book, and take out the special bookmark we placed inside the book. The bookmark was actually a raffle ticket that had to be filled out and tossed into the fishing net held by a stand-up mermaid located at the Circulation Desk. The mermaid was actually a life-sized cardboard stand-up of Marilyn Monroe which we outfitted with a blue-green foil fishtail, large paper rocks, and well-placed shells. She beckoned passersby to enter the raffle and to join us for the Magical Realism party. The prizes for the raffle, which we held during the party, were gift certificates to a local books and music store.

For the party, the library had to be transmogrified. We combined magic and reality both visually and logically in each major service area. The Circulation Desk became a giant leaping dolphin surrounded by blue, green, and clear Mylar with a large poster of the quote: "*Let the joy and inspiration of the dolphin lead us to a more positive and helpful world–uniting in spirit, humans and dolphins.*" The Reference Area was filled by a large (and very real) hot air balloon basket, replete with three 3-foot starry purple, orange, and green balloons, and a giant banner that read: *"C'mon Let Us Give Your Mind a Ride!"* (See Figure 4.) We also covered the area in green and blue tissue paper with yellow paper sunflowers and white clouds as the background. The newly-designed English As a Second Language area was engulfed by a Persian carpet and silky fabric. The poster for this area read, *"A well-composed book is a magic carpet on which we are wafted to a world that we cannot enter in any other way."*

The rest of the library was filled with giant, multi-colored leaves printed from our trustworthy color printer, two-foot wide yellow, orange, and green silk butterflies, and three dozen balloons in the corresponding colors of yellow, orange, purple, and green. The floors (and desk surfaces) were completely covered with neon colored feathers and at each entrance to the library we hung floor to ceiling multi-colored Mylar fringe curtains that tickled when you passed through. We were astounded by the number of books and films in our collection that were considered in the realm of "magical realism," and we displayed them all with colorful leafy posters describing the genre.

Each computer workstation was affixed with white, glittery wings and the end panels of the front stacks were turned into leafy trees with paper angels flying from the treetops. A yellow brick road (made from yellow construction paper) led guests from the entranceways to the coffee and food–which were equally magical–and plastic penguins standing atop large purple and gold foiled boxes greeted guests by reading books boldly entitled, *"Do You Believe In Magic?"*

We chose Paul McCartney's album *"Rushes"* (released under the pseudonym "The Fireman") as the party music–one of our staff members just has a knack for finding the right sound for a particular party–and positioned the CD player near the three urns of coffee which we turned into three castles offering up "vaporescent infusions," "intoxicating potions," and "nepenthean elixirs." The staff bakers created magic bars, handmade butterfly candies, bee bars emerging from a real hornet's nest, a large white cake decorated with silk butterflies and the word "IMAGINE," and other homemade baked goods and fruit designs with magical themes.

The morning of the party day, a large cardboard stand-up of Betty Grable, dressed in a Tunxis t-shirt, a rainbow Mylar "grass" skirt, feathers, balloons, greeted everyone passing the library. She held a large colorful poster inviting all to celebrate magical realism at a party that afternoon.

FIGURE 4. Hot Air Balloon Welcomes Party-Goers

PARTY AFTERGLOW

The ripple effect of the party atmosphere can be felt for weeks throughout the campus. Creating an event where the entire campus can come together in a spirit of camaraderie, cleverness, and fun creates positive energy for the college, as well as for the library. In some ways, it is purely social. When the party is in the library, people reacquaint themselves with the enjoyment of browsing new titles, perusing bestsellers and DVDs, and just relaxing in a comfortable, friendly, and stress-free environment. Our circulation statistics soar during the parties, as well as in the following weeks–as do requests for new materials. When our parties are out of the library, we get the chance to create outside the box and bring the distinctive spirit of the library with us. We also weather a fair amount of teasing about when we will be hosting the next party and just how we plan to top our previous efforts! You cannot put a price on this level of promotion.

THE SECRET TO OUR SUCCESS

The success of the library parties begins with the library team. Because we have the collective desire to create a great party for the college, that becomes our goal. According to authors Frank LaFasto and Carl Larson in their book, *When Teams Work Best*, "the single most important determinant of a team's success is a 'clear and elevating goal.' The goal is what it's all about; it is the reason the team exists." (2001, 72). The staff has to buy in, as a team, to the work it takes to host a creative party, one that will draw the campus community to the library, engage them intellectually, make them laugh and relax, and subtly showcase the services, personalities, and resources available. It is our way of jump-starting the semester in a positive and meaningful way, ensuring that the library captures the attention of the campus community right from the start.

To accomplish this task, the library staff gathers informally in the summer. We identify a time when all staff members are available and we keep the party as our only agenda item. Everyone who works in the library, from the student workers to the director, is given the opportunity to participate. As we begin this planning process, we are reminded of Helen Keller's words, "Alone we can do so little; together we can do so much."

Potential party themes usually emerge from one creative idea brought forth by a staff member who has an inspiration or sees a connection between a new library resource, a current event, something in popular culture, or even something silly (like moving the furniture). Knowing that we prefer themes that are intellectual, clever, and somehow connected to the library, a round robin of related ideas and discussion continues until we arrive at a party theme that resonates with all of us. At this point, we can usually tell that the theme is a winner because the ideas on food, implementation, colors, design, and surround flow easily. We also all agree that there needs to be an "aura of surprise" to the party. By now, the campus community members are reasonably sure that the library staff will be planning some kind of festive event for the fall semester, and part of the fun for us is keeping them guessing as to what and when it will be.

To the casual observer, this round robin of discussion may sound like chaos. However, to the contrary, we are extremely focused. LaFasto and Larson assert that "the ability of successful teams to focus energy on the goal can be observed in the processes they use for solving problems and making decisions. Successful teams have a more disciplined approach, which allows them to raise issues constructively, focus their energy on facts, and invite and reconcile differing perspectives, while their effort remains productive and aligned with the goal" (2001, 73). We stay aligned by realizing that we will not always "get it" the first time around. Sometimes we need a couple of these planning sessions to fine tune an idea or perhaps start over with a new conceptual thread before we can all commit to a theme. The planning can be as fun as the party itself, as it represents a time for everyone to relax and let ideas flow. Once we agree on a party theme, details begin falling in place.

This is where the team coalesces best–the individual talents of the staff surface and it is amazing to watch how animated people become when they have the opportunity to utilize their gifts in concert with the party theme. The creative directors outline the big picture, the designers see the colors and props, the bakers connect the theme with food, the technicians take charge of furniture placement, lights, and plugs, the collectors bring in items from home, the shoppers start surfing the Internet and dollar stores, the literati comb the collection for quotes and bibliographic representations, the graphic designers start creating displays, invitations, and posters, and the library director allows the team the freedom and breadth to "do their collective and individual thing" and most importantly, identifies the means for financing the operation.

This is a good time to mention the importance of hiring competent and complementary staff for an academic library. It is imperative that human resource directors and campus search committees take every opportunity to hire competent people who "fit" into the library team. LaFasto and Larson's research tells us that the first thing team members look for in a teammate is a core competency or a "working knowledge." This includes both experience and problem-solving ability. The second thing that team members look for are four "teamwork" qualities that signify success: (1) openness, (2) supportiveness, (3) action orientation or personal initiative, and (4) a positive personal style (2001, 5).

All four of these teamwork qualities play an important role in our successful party planning process. The openness of the team is critical in determining the party theme. We need to communicate regularly on intersecting details for the party, including ideas for décor, food, music, resources, design, logistics, and timing. The staff supports each other in implementing the party details by taking on the responsibility they are either best equipped to handle or most interested in tackling. Some staff members have more personal initiative than others at different points in the party planning, design, and delivery, but everyone is involved at the level he or she can be, and because the library has a positive ethos, that energy filters its way into any project undertaken. When we need to mobilize quickly right before party time, everyone is on board. Each library staff member takes pride in determining creative and innovative ways to get tasks done for the party. And because we are working with limited funds, there is a collective challenge to create a lively party atmosphere on a shoestring budget.

CREATING CAMPUS SPIRIT

"I am always amazed when people proudly proclaim, 'I never mix business with pleasure.' If you want to build a successful team at work, you should always mix business with pleasure. People like to do business with people who like doing business" (Weinstein 1996, 24).

We hear it all the time–people love the library. Student satisfaction surveys, alumni surveys, accreditation reports, and valedictorians' speeches all tout the personalized service, dedication, competency, and friendliness of the library staff. Many articles and books focus on the importance of collective vision in higher education, turning to management techniques such as total quality management (TQM) or quality improvement processes (QIP) as a means to achieving functionality, task completion, or cost savings benefits. Rarely does professional literature measure the importance of team spirit in promoting campus morale or raising the level of positive energy in a college. We believe that people enjoy "belonging" in an organization and revel in being a special element in something that is good. The library parties are designed to infuse the campus with a collective sense of caring, belonging, fun, and relaxation.

To attain this lofty goal we now operate on the following simple premises for our parties:

- The library staff shares the vision of creating a great party.
- We design an experience that most people will enjoy.
- We invite the college community—faculty, staff, administrators, and students.
- We personalize the invitation.
- We maintain our reputation by being painstakingly detailed.
- We keep the library open and all services available. It always amazes us how supportive and excited patrons can be when they see us setting up for a party.
- We allow each library staff member the opportunity to participate in every stage of the planning on whatever level he or she feels comfortable.
- We make sure invitees have a tangible "gift" to remind them of the library.
- We allow our guests the opportunity to drop the Sisyphean rock of teaching, researching, advising, typing, conferencing, counseling, tutoring, maintaining, and administering . . . and invite them to rock on.

We do get interrogated about our funding sources for these elaborate parties, and actually many of the props, refreshments, and decorations come from either the home collections of staff or from some very ingenious shopping at dollar stores and discount houses. We also do a lot of our own signage and design work on our computers with the aid of a very trusty color printer. For pricier items, such as the fortune cookies or stress balls, we have a small, donated stipend of money from a very appreciative community patron who requested that we use the money for special events or small improvements to the library. That, added to the gifts of $5 or $10 that other appreciative patrons have donated, helps to defray the cost of trinkets and theme-related larger items.

IS IT WORTH ALL THE WORK?

As corny as it sounds, we always get back what we give out. The true element of our party success is the care we take to make each one enthusiastically personal and also collectively rich. We want the campus community to know that we value being part of their lives and by wrapping the cerebral with a lot of fun, people respond positively by attending our parties in droves. What we get back is tremendous support from our colleagues, sometimes in the form of campus awards or personal notes, but also by a renewed interest in our collection and our services, a rise in circulation, positive feedback in student surveys, personal satisfaction, communal membership, and a creative outlet for our staff members–particularly those staff members who thrive on creativity in the workplace.

DO WE JUST WANT TO PARTY ALL THE TIME?

Well, no. We admit it. The parties are really hard work. There are times when staff members are spending much of their free time shopping, baking, creating decorations, remembering items from home, relentlessly printing signs and posters, and making endless to-do lists. On party day, we are so focused on set-up that we can barely answer a reference question. At the end of the parties, we are drained. And there have been some glitches in some of our more outlandish decisions. The rented champagne fountain left a sticky residue of soda spray at the Reference Desk for months. We accidentally threw out the insides of the giant coffee pot when discarding the coffee grounds. One Librarian thoughtfully snipped a collection of roadside wildflowers for table centerpieces, only to find that she had unknowingly invited a bee colony to join her on her commute. Yet another Librarian was kind enough to pick up donuts (the focus of our party's food fare!) on a morning that happened to coincide with a freakish snow and ice storm. She did it without incident, but it was a harrowing excursion. The director schlepped through a driving rainstorm to pick up a special order of honey wheat baguettes that were so fresh from the oven they had to be laid out on large flat plans and covered with plastic wrap to stay dry. The baguettes escaped sogginess, but the director was not as lucky. We have weathered some unfortunate coffee and punch spills, and we've blown a few circuit breakers. All in all, however, it has been well worth the effort–though there is always the post-party lingering question . . . what can we come up with for next year?

QUICK BIB

Cohen, Shari S. 1987. Mixing business with pleasure. *Business Marketing* 72 (7): 95-97.

LaFasto, Frank, and Carl Larson. 2001. *When teams work best.* Thousand Oaks, CA: Sage Publications.

Seymour, Rhea. 2004. November. A party that means business. *Profit* 23 (5): 83-85.

REFERENCES

Cohen, Shari S. 1987. Mixing business with pleasure. *Business Marketing* 72 (7): 95-97.

LaFasto, Frank, and Carl Larson. 2001. *When teams work best.* Thousand Oaks, CA: Sage Publications.

Lavoie, Lisa. 2002. Throwing a party to meet all of our patrons' needs. *MLS: Marketing Library Services.* 16 (5): 1-3.

Seymour, Rhea. 2004. A party that means business. *Profit* 23 (5): 83-85.

Weinstein, Matt. 1996. Managing to have fun. *Psychology Today* 29 (4): 24.

Index

Academic libraries. *See also* individual
academic library
audiences of, 36
continuing education resources for
marketing, 89-90
Internet resources for marketing,
87-89
literature analyzing promotion of,
31
lobbying and, 59-60
marketing in, 48-49,82,154
photographing events at, 42-43
programs and exhibits for, 36-37
public information offices, 40
resource guides for marketing,
83-84
resources for promoting new
services, 84-86
reviewing publicity of other, 43
summary about, 61
vendor resources for marketing,
86-87
Advertising. *See also* Publicity
direct, 75
paid, 75
After-the-fact publicity, 42-43
Alumni, as external audience, 56-57
American University, 2
American University Library, 2-3
assessment at, 2-3
reflections on, 10-12
focus groups at, 4-5
application of findings of, 8-10
data analysis of, 7-8
methodology used for, 5-6
reflections on, 10-12
LibQUAL+survey at, 3-5

Assessment
culture of, at American University
Library, 2
libraries and, 2
reflections on, 10-12
@ your library, 21
Audiences
brainstorming worksheet for library
hours reduction and, 64
communications grid for matching
media to, 63
external, 56-61
internal, 55-56
of Milner Library, 54

Brainstorming worksheet, library hours
reduction, 64
Branding virtual reference services,
69-70

Calendars, community, 42
Chat reference services, marketing,
66-67
Coates Library (Trinity University),
Frankenstein exhibit at
developing programming ideas for,
103-104
educational component of, 107-109
enlisting help for, 104
evaluation of, 114-116
funding for, 110-114
fun events for, 110
publicity for, 104-107
reasons for, 102-103
Collaboration, virtual reference and,
72-73

BOOK ORDER FORM!

Order a copy of this book with this form or online at:
http://www.HaworthPress.com/store/product.asp?sku=5765

Real-Life Marketing and Promotion Strategies in College Libraries
Connecting with Campus and Community

___ in softbound at $22.95 ISBN-13: 978-0-7890-3158-7 / ISBN-10: 0-7890-3158-2.
___ in hardbound at $42.95 ISBN-13: 978-0-7890-3157-0 / ISBN-10: 0-7890-3157-4.

COST OF BOOKS _____

POSTAGE & HANDLING _____
US: $4.00 for first book & $1.50
for each additional book
Outside US: $5.00 for first book
& $2.00 for each additional book.

SUBTOTAL _____

In Canada: add 7% GST. _____

STATE TAX _____
CA, IL, IN, MN, NJ, NY, OH, PA & SD residents
please add appropriate local sales tax.

FINAL TOTAL _____

If paying in Canadian funds, convert
using the current exchange rate,
UNESCO coupons welcome.

❑ BILL ME LATER:
Bill-me option is good on US/Canada/
Mexico orders only; not good to jobbers,
wholesalers, or subscription agencies.

❑ Signature _____

❑ Payment Enclosed: $ _____

❑ PLEASE CHARGE TO MY CREDIT CARD:
❑ Visa ❑ MasterCard ❑ AmEx ❑ Discover
❑ Diner's Club ❑ Eurocard ❑ JCB

Account # _____

Exp Date _____

Signature _____

(Prices in US dollars and subject to change without notice.)

PLEASE PRINT ALL INFORMATION OR ATTACH YOUR BUSINESS CARD

Name	
Address	
City	State/Province Zip/Postal Code
Country	
Tel	Fax
E-Mail	

May we use your e-mail address for confirmations and other types of information? ❑ Yes ❑ No We appreciate receiving
your e-mail address. Haworth would like to e-mail special discount offers to you, as a preferred customer.
We will never share, rent, or exchange your e-mail address. We regard such actions as an invasion of your privacy.

Order from your **local bookstore** or directly from
The Haworth Press, Inc. 10 Alice Street, Binghamton, New York 13904-1580 • USA
Call our toll-free number (1-800-429-6784) / Outside US/Canada: (607) 722-5857
Fax: 1-800-895-0582 / Outside US/Canada: (607) 771-0012
E-mail your order to us: orders@HaworthPress.com

For orders outside US and Canada, you may wish to order through your local
sales representative, distributor, or bookseller.
For information, see http://HaworthPress.com/distributors

(Discounts are available for individual orders in US and Canada only, not booksellers/distributors.)

The Haworth Press, Inc.

Please photocopy this form for your personal use.
www.HaworthPress.com

BOF05